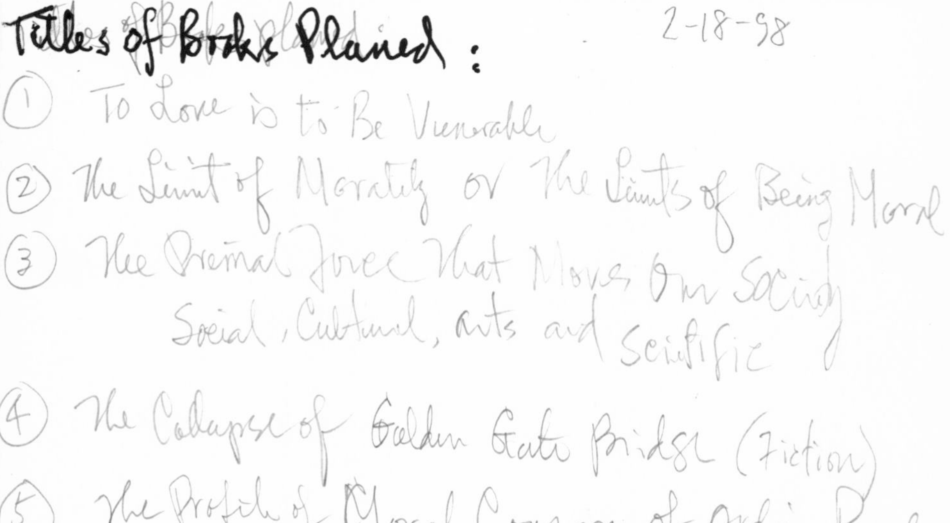

Titles of Books Planed: 2-18-98

1. To Love is to Be Vunerable
2. The Limit of Moratily or The Limits of Being Moral
3. The Primal Force That Moves Our Socity Social, Cultural, arts and Scintific
4. The Collapse of Golden Gate Bridge (Fiction)
5. The Profile of Moral Courage of Ordiny People

Charm Intact

People generally want to avert their eyes from the sight of those dealing with overwhelming physical challenges. But **CHRISTOPHER REEVE** won't let us. Reeve's book *Still Me* lodges itself at No. 1 on various best-seller lists. No wonder. By the day of his book-launch party, Reeve had already appeared on the *Late Show with David Letterman* (who, oddly, did not use the opportunity for a guest-specific Top 10 list), the *Today* show, *Oprah*, *20/20* and *Larry King Live* and done countless print interviews. Writing the book, Reeve says, "was one of the highlights of my life, before and after the acci[illegible] still can't eat, breathe or do al[illegible] own. But he ca[illegible]

Time 5/25/98

6-23-98

The word "shero" is introduced on KQED Michael Krasny's show to mean "hero" in the female sense. A book is published with title "Sheros".

A caller suggested the word "history" be changed to, or added one, "herstory".

Is this gender thing really necessary?

Varla Venturas (?) author's name.

HOW TO WRITE

To Paul —

Richard Rhodes

ALSO BY RICHARD RHODES

FICTION

Sons of Earth

The Last Safari

Holy Secrets

The Ungodly

VERITY

Dark Sun

Nuclear Renewal

Making Love

A Hole in the World

Farm

The Making of the Atomic Bomb

Looking for America

The Ozarks

The Inland Ground

HOW TO WRITE

Advice and Reflections

RICHARD RHODES

WILLIAM MORROW AND COMPANY, INC.
NEW YORK

It is the policy of William Morrow and Company, Inc., and its imprints and affiliates, recognizing the importance of preserving what has been written, to print the books we publish on acid-free paper, and we exert our best efforts to that end.

Library of Congress Cataloging-in-Publication Data

Rhodes, Richard.
How to write : advice and reflections / Richard Rhodes.
p. cm.
Includes index.
ISBN 0-688-14095-5
1. Authorship. I. Title.
PN147.R57 1995
808'.02—dc20 94-45342
CIP

Printed in the United States of America

First Edition

1 2 3 4 5 6 7 8 9 10

BOOK DESIGN BY BRIAN MULLIGAN

For

ANNE SIBBALD

CONTENTS

HOW
TO
WRITE

'WORDS LIKE A LIFE ROPE'

If you want to write, you can. Fear stops most people from writing, not lack of talent, whatever that is. Who am I? What right have I to speak? Who will listen to me if I do? You're a human being, with a unique story to tell, and you have every right. If you speak with passion, many of us will listen. We need stories to live, all of us. We live by story. Yours enlarges the circle.

There are more ways to tell a story than there are stories to tell; a story is a map, and maps always simplify. You write a story whenever you put words on paper—even filling in a license form. A love letter or a business letter, a novel or a narrative, a short story or a news story, a screenplay, a song lyric, a family or scholarly history, a legal brief, a technical manual, a biography or an autobiography, a personal journal, a scientific paper, a photo caption, an essay, a poem, a sermon, advertising copy, schoolwork—all these and many others are forms of story you may wish to write.

The challenge is to get from where you are to where you want to be. That probably won't be easy or quick. Writing is work, hard work, and its rewards are personal more than financial, which means most people have to do it after hours. But if writing is work, learning to write isn't necessarily painful. To the contrary, silence is pain that writing relieves. Our uniqueness isolates us. Writing, we make our way out of our isolation onto the commons that we share. It's an emotional experience. You stumble gibbering into the valley of the shadow; you pull yourself hand over hand to ecstatic heights. Beyond those terrific passages gathers the community of readers, an open, world community of people—men, women, and children—who want and need to hear.

Writing is only one kind of making. Loving, raising children, doing the work that buys our groceries, are kinds of making as well. But because writing is structured from a common code, it's more durable than the private events that fill our lives. Books know no hierarchy and abolish space and time. We read Montaigne and know what it was like to be Montaigne, four hundred years ago, and may at least hope that someone will read us and know us four hundred years hence. Only temples and pyramids enjoy such permanence as writing enjoys. Human memory is the only certain immortality; books are memory's hard copy. Presidents and royals may read your work, your great-grandchildren, devoted fans in Red Rock, Arizona, or Timbuktu. The *Iliad* has been sung for three thousand years.

Writers are people who write. If you need a place to begin, begin there. Years ago, I came off active duty in the United States Air Force with a pregnant wife and one hundred dollars to my name. I was living in Kansas City at the time and found work at Hallmark Cards, writing the daily employee newspaper. A poet who made his living teaching English told me scornfully that such writing was drivel and I'd be better off driving a cab. But five mornings a week by 10 A.M. I had to fill two sides of an 8½-by-11 sheet of paper with news—of promotions and retirements, of corporate doings, of births and marriages and deaths. The forms of the stories I wrote were highly stylized, the contents carefully censored, but every morning by 10 A.M. I had to get the Spam to the front line. At Yale I had chosen not to take the only creative writing course the university offered, which was called Daily Themes and which required a page of original writing delivered to the instructor's door every morning, five days a week. Now Hallmark was paying me to double that production. (The poet would say there's no comparison. He'd be wrong. Every form you learn to write, no matter how mundane, is another tool in your kit.) I worked in the Hallmark public relations department for a man named Conrad Knickerbocker, the public relations manager, who had already begun publishing book reviews and fiction. After I got to know Knick a little, I asked him timidly how you become a writer. He said more pungently what I wrote at the beginning of this paragraph. He said, "Rhodes, you apply ass to chair." I call that solid-gold advice the Knickerbocker Rule.

But I was afraid, as you may be afraid. Who was I? What right had I to speak? My fear manifested itself as creative paralysis. In those days I was trying to write fiction. I could write the Hallmark employee newspaper, the sales bulletin, the employee magazine, and product press releases day in, day out almost without faltering, but if I began a short story or worked on a novel in the evening at home I drifted into trance states and couldn't push through, couldn't continue and finish. I had writer's block before I became a writer. Nor was the quality of what I was writing even close to what I wanted it to be. I wrote Joycean or Faulknerian pastiches; when I tried to write in my own voice I overworked my sentences to the point of affectation. I was three hands clapping. I was too tight.

My immediate personal problem was post-traumatic stress disorder left over from a time of childhood abuse. You may not suffer from such a condition, but many people who want to write have difficulties getting started similar to mine. I know because I notice their response in the audience when I lecture about writing and mention fear: they look relieved. Most of us were punished for telling stories when we were children, which inhibited verbal invention with a flinch of shame. We learned in school that the rules of language are rigid and the standards of literature insurmountably high. So we storied away effortlessly among ourselves but went blank when the teacher asked us to open our notebooks and write. Unless you're a paragon of self-confidence, such conditioning has its effect on you. Nor does society encourage the buoyant hypnotic state where the creative imagination floats. I was a little worse. I was afraid that if I let out my rage I would somehow destroy the world.

Writing was the answer for me. Somewhere within me I seem to have known that. If you want to write, you may feel that writing is the answer for you as well. I find at least partial explanation for this sense of calling in the literature of suffering. The suffering such works report is extreme and the power of narrative therapeutic, as I will illustrate, but even at everyday levels of experience or up along the curve at the other extreme of celebration, the process of writing is always a healing process because the function of creation is always, *always,* the alleviation of pain—the writer's, first of all, and then the pain of those who read what she has written. Imagination is compassionate. Writing is a form of making, and making humanizes the world.[1]

Thus, in his extraordinary book, *Achilles in Vietnam,* about treating Vietnam veterans for combat post-traumatic stress disorder, the physician Jonathan Shay reports that narrative heals:

> Severe trauma explodes the cohesion of consciousness. When a survivor creates fully realized narrative that brings together the shattered knowledge of what happened, the emotions that were aroused by the meaning of the events, and the bodily sensations that the physical events created, the survivor pieces back together the fragmentation of consciousness that trauma has caused. Such narrative often results in the remission of some

symptoms. . . . Narrative enables the survivor to rebuild the ruins of character.[2]

The concentration camp survivor and psychotherapist Viktor Frankl, in a book I cherish, *Man's Search for Meaning*, quotes Spinoza to wider and more general effect: "Emotion, which is suffering, ceases to be suffering as soon as we form a clear and precise picture of it."[3] Spinoza's "clear and precise" picture was rational, but Frankl has something more phenomenal in mind: the discovery of a meaning that gives us reason to want to live even in extremity. He quotes Nietzsche: "He who has a *why* to live for can bear with almost any *how*."[4] That tragic and courageous insight saved Frankl from despair at Auschwitz and Dachau, as he describes in his book. He applies Nietzsche's aphorism concretely, and his application sounds like Jonathan Shay's "narrative":

> It is impossible to define the meaning of life in a general way. Questions about the meaning of life can never be answered by sweeping statements. "Life" does not mean something vague, but something very real and concrete, just as life's tasks are also very real and concrete. They form man's destiny, which is different and unique for each individual. No man and no destiny can be compared with any other man or any other destiny. No situation repeats itself, and each situation calls for a different response.[5]

Why resides in *how*, and *how* is highly specific. "Life," Frankl sums up, "ultimately means taking the responsibility to find the right answer to its problems and to fulfill the tasks which it constantly sets for each individual." Life is action, that is, not abstraction. All these statements apply to writing as well—not surprising, since writing is a simulation of life. (Which is why good writing doesn't spell out morals; life doesn't either.)

One more version of writing as alleviation. The journalist Roger Rosenblatt, thrown together in Nairobi in 1994 with a group of colleagues preparing to report on the slaughter that year in Rwanda, found himself analyzing how he and they dealt with the recurring inhumanity they saw. He identifies three stages of response: shock and revulsion and "a twinge of guilty excitement"; then bitterness and spite and hatred of "the people on whom they report"; then a third stage, during which they no longer believed that their reporting would improve the situation but found "something mysteriously redeeming in the telling." Rosenblatt mentions a Norwegian colleague named Gunnar Kopperud who felt himself breaking down at a Mauritanian refugee camp. How did you pull yourself out? Rosenblatt asked Kopperud. "I started taking notes," the Norwegian told him. "That small ordinary act gave me purpose. If those people didn't have a future, well, I did. I wrote, and I used the words like a life rope."[6] He who has a *why* to live for can bear with almost any *how*.

I broke through to serious writing, by which I mean writing that knew and felt and sensed, only after I began a long course of psychotherapy in my thirty-second year. Shay found similarly that victims of combat post-traumatic stress disorder had to establish their "safety, sobriety, and self-care" as an essential precondition of healing.[7] I was anorexic and emotionally numbed; six months into therapy, with a strong positive transference established, I stopped feinting at suicide, started eating, and started writing. I wrote about the killing of coyotes and cocks for sport in rural Kansas, a violence that seemed to match my own. That first work of essay was one of my best. *Esquire* bought it and published it with stunning photographs by Art Kane of fighting cocks brandishing steel malevolent spurs.

But of course "Death All Day in Kansas" wasn't an immaculate conception. I'd written for years (including the Hallmark *Noon News* years) before I wrote it, or I couldn't have taken advantage of the emotional breakthrough.[8] I'd practiced every way I could, however journeywork the results. And before I began writing and while I was practicing I studied writing, consciously and unconsciously, just as you almost certainly have done. I studied writing by reading. I'd been reading, ardently and even compulsively, since I was four.

Reading is the one necessary prerequisite for writing. Every published writer of books I know grew up reading. It's obvious that entertainers like Liza Minnelli, who were born into show business, have an advantage over entertainers who try to break in as adults. It's a rare theoretical physicist whose father and/or mother wasn't an academic, positioning the physicist well up the ladder of abstract thought. Successful farmers, believe me, are almost always born to the trade. Any complicated human activity benefits from childhood apprenticeship; the sooner you begin, the more you're likely to learn and practice and therefore the better you're likely to be. If the preferred form of expressive discourse among young people today is the screenplay, that's probably because young people today grow up watching movies and television more than reading. Not many years ago the preferred form was poetry. When I was in college, in the 1950s, the preferred form was the short story. I grew up on books, so it was always books I wanted to write, not short stories or poems or screenplays, though I've tried my hand at all three to see how they work. All the craft of books is found in books. Not the life—the craft.

If you're a serious and dedicated reader, then, you already know part of how to write. You know the forms and conventions of writing and how others have used those forms and conventions to shape their work. (If you haven't been a reader, I'd suggest you become one fast if you want to write.) What you may not know is how to begin and continue and finish, and how to publish when you're done. This book can help.

Which brings me back to fear. The fear that grips someone who wants to write is usually not undifferentiated and monolithic but a composite of smaller fears. With time and thought, some can be resolved; others can be shooed back under their rocks or even coaxed into harness and put to work. Stephen LaBerge, a scientist who studies sleep, told me once about a successful encounter with nightmare. LaBerge teaches and studies lucid dreaming, a state of sleep during which one wakes up, so to speak, within one's dream and takes control as actively as a film director controls the making of a film. Dreaming one night that a monster was chasing him, LaBerge went lucid, turned around, and hugged the monster, which immediately ceased to threaten him. His dream experience left LaBerge feeling blissful. "The monster was my own invention, after all," he told me, "part of my personality. In the dream I acknowledged it and accepted it. That kind of reintegration ought to feel good."

I was afraid that my rage would destroy the world. The time came when I had a contract to write a novel, my first work of fiction and my second book (later I'll explain how I got there). Not surprisingly, I had proposed a historical novel about the Donner Party, those midwestern pioneers who went west to California in 1846 but were trapped in the Sierra Nevada by early snow and survived by eating their dead. Apparently the subject matter wasn't sufficiently grisly to placate the rage I felt at having been beaten, starved, and tortured when I was a child. Before I could write the Donner Party novel, I disgorged another fiction, a one-hundred-forty-page novella I wrote in one maniacal week, an indirect first-person narrative of the childhood of a Lee Harvey Oswald–like assassin (a childhood like my own). I insisted that my agent offer *Assassin* for publication. He did, perhaps handling it with tongs. He refused to tell me what the dozen editors said to whom he sent it. He quoted only one, the kindest of the lot; she told him, "I think it's perfectly dreadful." I don't believe my little story is dreadful; in its own way it's as fine a crafted object as a long brass rifle shell, but it makes *Last Exit to Brooklyn* look demure. It's still on the shelf, unpublished. It didn't destroy the world, and since the world went on revolving, I went on to write *The Ungodly*.

I started therapy for myself, not for writing, but it was through that process that the breakthrough came. Talking to someone who's trained to listen isn't a bad idea if you want to be a writer. It's another experience of narrative. Franz Kafka rejected psychoanalysis because he feared that exorcising his demons would exorcise his angels as well; but my angels taught my demons to sing. Seven years of therapy was no more expensive than graduate school would have been, and I've come to think of therapy as graduate school for the emotions (or was it remedial?). When I groaned at the expense, my therapist, a good man trained at the Menninger Clinic, expressed the hope that therapy would pay for itself. Since I've made a good living writing now for more than twenty years, it did.

You may not carry so much freight that you need therapy. You may not even be interested in "creative" writing; you may have read this far to see what you can pick up to help you as a journalist, in business, or even writing a *Noon News*. Whatever your purpose, the best remedy for fear of writing, any kind of writing, is the Knickerbocker Rule: ass to chair. If you're afraid you can't write, the answer is to write. Every sentence you construct adds weight to the balance pan. If you're afraid of what other people will think of your efforts, don't show them until you write your way beyond your fear. If writing a book is impossible, write a chapter. If writing a chapter is impossible, write a page. If writing a page is impossible, write a paragraph. If writing a paragraph is impossible, write a sentence. If writing even a sentence is impossible, write a word and teach yourself everything there is to know about that word and then write another, connected word and see where their connection leads. A page a day is a book a year. Listen to that again: a page a day is a book a year. You may not yet be ready even for a page, much less a book. But you can certainly begin with a word. Write your name. Do you love it? Do you hate it? Who gave it to you and why? What's in a name? Tell me a story. Once upon a time . . .

When the fear is upon you, write for yourself. It doesn't matter what you write as long as you do it regularly. Set aside an hour or a half hour daily or as often as you can. If you don't think you have time, keep a record of how you spend the quarter hours of your day and see where you can borrow (most people spend most of their time outside of working hours watching television). Steal an hour from sleep on alternate early mornings if there's no other choice.

Use writing equipment you're comfortable with—a pencil, a pen, a typewriter, a computer. You don't need to keep a formal journal. The less baggage, the better. The point is to strip away every possible constraint except the fear itself, so to find your way around your fear. You and your fear, wrestling like Jacob and the angel. Jacob did all right despite the odds.

Forget spelling. Shakespeare spelled his own name four different ways. Forget punctuation if paying attention to it inhibits you—you can always add it later. Gertrude Stein wrote with minimal punctuation. She said people know where the commas go. She wanted her writing to flow, to reproduce the way her thought seemed to flow, so she borrowed some of the metric devices of poetry. Here she explores what I called our unique stories, our personal histories:

> A history of any one must be a long one, slowly it comes out of them from their beginning to their ending, slowly you can see it in them the nature and the mixtures in them, slowly everything comes out from each one in the kind of repeating each one does in the different parts and kinds of living they have in them,

> slowly then the history of them comes out from them, slowly then any one who looks well at any one will have the history of the whole of that one. Slowly the history of each one comes out of each one. Sometime then there will be a history of every one.[9]

You're letting your history out. That may be one reason you're afraid. If you don't want anyone to read it, you can always delete it from your disk or tear it up.

Your thought may not flow like Gertrude Stein's. You. May. Want. To. Write. Like. This. At. First. Feel free. Don't think about how you're writing: write. Everyone knows how to do something: describe a process. How do you tie your shoe? How do you brush your teeth? How do you plant a bulb, drive a car, read a map? Everyone has feelings: how do you feel about something or someone? Set a mirror before you and describe your face. Describe your hands. Are they different or the same? Language itself may have come out of our hands, the left hand holding (if you're right-handed): a noun; the right hand manipulating: a verb. What do your hands have to say to each other? Describe what you smell, sitting wherever you are. Describe what you taste or hear or see. What parts of you touch the world? Where does the world touch you? How does it feel? What are you thinking? Write it down. What do you think about what you were thinking? Write that down. Write until your time is up. Put your writing away.

Start again next time: write about something else. Write something deep. Write something silly. Write your first memory. Write the most revealing story you know about your mother, your father, your lover, your boss, your teacher, your child. Write two people talking. Write a joke. Write a beginning. Write an ending. Write a middle. You are a camera. You are a child. You are an avenging angel. You pant and gasp with love in someone's arms. You clot with black hate. You yearn. You're happy. You're sad. Write yearning, happiness, sadness, *concretely* as acts—things you do, not things you think or feel. You are a soul. Here is what you are and what these episodes of writing are about:

> *There was a child went forth every day,*
> *And the first object he look'd upon, that object he became,*
> *and that object became part of him for the day*
> *or a certain part of the day,*
> *Or for many years or stretching cycles of years.*
>
> *The early lilacs became part of this child,*
> *And grass and white and red morning-glories,*
> *and white and red clover,*
> *and the song of the phoebe-bird,*
> *And the Third-month lambs and the sow's pink-faint litter,*
> *and the mare's foal and the cow's calf,*
> *And the noisy brood of the barnyard or by the mire*
> *of the pond-side,*
> *And the fish suspending themselves so curiously below there,*
> *and the beautiful curious liquid,*
> *And the water-plants with their graceful flat heads,*
> *all became part of him. . . .*[10]

No one makes craft, carefully wrought, seem more casual than Walt Whitman. What your episodes are about is opening that fresh, innocent eye.

None of this work will be wasted. At the very least you'll learn from it. If you're as frugal as most writers I know, you'll probably use it later.

If even these first efforts make you fearful, move them into a comfortable frame: write them in a letter to a person you trust and file the letter (or mail it, if you prefer). Tom Wolfe wrote his first *Esquire* piece as a letter to his editor. I suspect he chose that approach because the pomp of writing a magazine piece was inhibiting. All the editor had to do was delete the salutation.

Writing moves you into a place of intense concentration similar to the concentration of chess and other complex games but more richly colored with feeling. It's like the place where you go mentally when you read, but it's lucid reading, so to speak, like lucid dreaming—you write the text you're reading. So choose your setting carefully. As you reinforce your writerly concentration by repetition, you're likely to reinforce your associations with your surroundings as well. Newly hatched ducklings imprint on the first moving object they see. That's wiring, not association, but the results can be comparably awkward. I heard of an ostrich once that fell in love with a two-hundred-watt bulb. Somewhere, years ago, I read that a famous European writer had to smell the cider of an apple core in his wastebasket in order to start writing. If such a harmless trigger helps, by all means use one. Marcel Proust expressed the multiple volumes of his *Remembrance of Things Past* from the taste of a madeleine.

I asked Kurt Vonnegut, Jr., once if he had an apple-core equivalent. He said, "A carton of Pall Malls and a fit of coughing." I got drunk to write at first. I thought I needed to, and maybe I did. Alcohol allays anxiety and loosens inhibition. But eventually I had to learn to write without alcohol. "Gosh," my therapist said dryly one day when he thought I was ready to hear it. "It's hard enough to write; it must be even harder when you're drunk." I found out it was, but switching over took a while, just as learning to write without smoking did. Ernest Hemingway used the nice trick of always stopping the previous day at a point where he knew what came next. Then he had a bridge.

If you're lucky, you finally learn simply to sit down and begin. Someone told the great British physicist Ernest Rutherford, who discovered the atomic nucleus, that he'd been lucky to come along at just the time he did in the development of his science. "Yes," he shot right back, "but I made my luck, didn't I." Make your luck. Sit down and begin.

Two

TOOLS

While you're writing freely, without intention, wrestling with your demons and your angels, let's talk about tools.

Writing is a craft. Its primary function is communication. I mean "craft" strictly: like carpentry or pottery, writing is handmade. Like other crafts as well, writing can sometimes be organized to the special depth and resonance people call art. Art is a curious, ill-defined, and elusive combination of craft and invention; with the exception of so-called primitive artists (who are really self-taught and who are much rarer in writing than in the visual arts), writers who would make art have to learn writing as a craft first. The best way to learn is by doing—and thinking about what you're doing while you're doing it. You wouldn't expect to make superior pottery the first time you sat down at a wheel. People often assume they know how to write because they know how to speak. There are deep and important connections between spoken and written language, but they're not the same thing. If you think they are, tape a conversation and transcribe it verbatim and see how it reads. Better to imagine that you'll be writing in a foreign language of which, at the outset, you know only a few words and only the rudiments of syntax.

I had the privilege several years ago of working with a Nobel laureate physicist named Luis W. Alvarez, editing his memoir, *Alvarez: Adventures of a Physicist.* At Berkeley in the 1930s, Luie helped develop the particle accelerator known as the cyclotron—the first really powerful instrument for studying atoms by bombarding them with accelerated atomic particles—and he subsequently worked on the atomic bomb. In 1980, he and his geologist son, Walter, formulated the theory, now well accepted, that an asteroid impacted the earth sixty-five million years ago and caused an "impact winter" of darkness and cold that killed off the dinosaurs. Luie's physical discoveries as well as his many inventions drew on his encyclopedic knowledge of isotopes, the variant physical forms of elements, and particularly radioactive isotopes, which give off types and intensities of radiation as unique as fingerprints. Luie knew the physical characteristics of the elements and their isotopes as well as he knew the back of his hand; it was because he knew them so well that he could apply their different qualities to his work. He and his son deduced their impact theory from a piece of rock no larger than a pack of cigarettes; their deduction depended upon knowing that the element iridium is rare in the earth's crust but plentiful in asteroids and comets. I asked Luie how he came to know isotopes so well. He told me that he learned them in his years on the night shift running the Berkeley cyclotron. For a while it was the only cyclotron in the world, and Luie's colleagues took advantage of that fact to make previously unknown radioactive isotopes right and left. Everyone claimed an element and got easy credit producing and reporting its radioactive isotopes. Luie was after bigger fish, but he participated in the isotope work, adjusting the cyclotron beam, arranging the target, feeling in his bones how much to crank up the current on the cranky instrument, where to jam in a metal shim to focus its magnetic field. On a wall in the laboratory the young physicists put up a big board laid out with the periodic table, with hooks projecting from the boxes designating elements, and each time someone identified a new isotope, Luie labeled a wooden tag with the isotope's characteristics and hung the tag from the appropriate hook. That's how he got to know isotopes so well. The knowledge he derived from those hard early years of work stayed with him like a vocabulary for the rest of his life. If you're starting out writing, you'll be working on the night shift; words, like unknown isotopes, will reveal their characteristics to you if you pay them close attention.

The tools of writing are a recording surface (paper, computer screen), a recording device (pencil, typewriter, keyboard/program), characters that stand for sounds or words, and a language. It's fortunate that the hardware of writing is so simple, because the software—language—is immensely complex, a vast, informal program of meaningful human sounds that developed historically and continues to evolve.

One property of language that bears significantly on writing is redundancy. You can say something many different ways. "Down the block and around the corner," "down the street and right at the corner," and "east to the next corner and then south" will all get you to the same place. The basic directional information is redundant across the three phrases. But the phrases aren't identical. In particular, the third phrase orients its directions by compass points. Country people give directions that way in the United States; city people usually don't. If a character in a story you were writing said "east to the next corner and then south," you might be signaling your readers that the character's background was rural. ("East to yonder corner . . ." would make the signal even clearer.)

Language evolved redundancy so that it could work at many different levels of precision. Infants learning to speak typically construct one-word sentences, then learn to make two-word sentences, and continue adding on as they progress. They usually become intelligible to their mothers and fathers first; at some point further along the way, even before their speech becomes standard, an attentive stranger can understand them. Most people speak less precisely than they write. They insert markers in their speech like "you know" or "uh" to give themselves time to think, markers that would be distracting in writing; in the rush of speech they use words loosely; they repeat themselves, for emphasis or to make sure their listeners understand them. In a personal letter or an E-mail message, people may not bother to check the meaning or the spelling of a questionable word and may use slang, odd punctuation, or casual grammar that they might not use in writing—which suggests that they craft informal writing more like speech, knocking up something temporary in pine. A first written draft is usually less precise than a finished text, because even seasoned professional writers do not find it easy to control simultaneously all the many disparate elements that enter into composition and usually pay more attention at first to roughing in basic elements rather than to word choice or sentence structure. A finished text written under deadline pressure—a paper for a class, a newspaper story—may be rougher in form and less precise than a text written at leisure. Even finished texts differ in quality, of course, depending primarily on the knowledge, skill, and finesse of the writer.

I bring up these points, which you may find obvious, because many people who want to write and many students think of "creative" writing primarily as self-expression, meaning unedited free association. Free-associating on paper is valuable—letting loose, as I described in the last chapter, and writing whatever you feel like writing, any way you want. It's valuable when you're learning to write to help you deal with fear, and it continues to be a useful technique for starting a piece of writing or moving beyond a point where you're stuck. It's a good way to develop characters and story by drawing on unconscious associations, free-associating *about* something (a process that used to be called meditation before meditation came to mean emptying your mind).

Some people cherish the spontaneity of their free-associative "self-expression" and resist editing it. For themselves, privately, they may be right to do so. Their personal writing may create a space of freedom for ecstatic expression in their lives; rereading their writing then recalls to them the feelings that creating it produced, just as hearing a cherished voice does or returning to a cherished place. Such states of mind can be fragile; editing might well shatter them. Personal writing is no one's business but yours.

Writing to communicate is a different matter. Professional writers, without exception so far as I know, consider unstructured, unedited free association to be at best only the first stage of writing. Not even Jack Kerouac wrote that way, although he tried to make it look as if he did. Gertrude Stein, the exception that proves the rule, seems to have practiced a kind of automatic writing. Some of it is extraordinary, but most of it is nearly unintelligible and has found only a small audience; the books by which Stein is known to a wider audience were heavily edited by her companion, Alice B. Toklas.

If you look at your unedited free association closely—look up the definitions and histories of key words, think through the sense of the sentences—you'll probably find that it doesn't always say what you thought you were saying when you wrote it. The brain plays tricks. Language is redundant partly to communicate despite those tricks. I interviewed a mathematician named Stanislaw Ulam once, one of the coinventors of the hydrogen bomb. He had recently returned from a conference on memory. He had decided, he told me, that memory was like a hound dog. You send it sniffing off to find something, and sooner or later it comes back with its quarry. Since then I've called my memory my dog. "My dog's looking for that," I tell my wife when I can't remember a name or think of a word. My dog is either overanxious to please or lazy. It brings back approximations—the first word it can find that seems to match. And the match categories are curious, a window into the way the brain (or at least my brain) stores words. I'm looking for the word "apple" and my dog comes panting back with "pear." I'm looking for the word "barn" and it brings back "berm." "Principal" fetches "principle," "cabinet" fetches "closet." If I were writing and I wrote these retrievals down in the heat of composition, I'd need to fix them later. That's one reason for editing. Writing communicates most effectively when it's carefully crafted.

Writing is made of words. Words are remarkable objects. Each one is a palimpsest, of which the electronic edition of my *American Heritage Dictionary* says the following:

> n. A written document, typically on vellum or parchment, that has been written upon several times, often with remnants of earlier, imperfectly erased writing still visible. Remnants of this kind are a major source for the recovery of lost literary works of classical antiquity. [Lat. *palimpsestus* < Gk. *palimpsēstos,* scraped again : *palin,* again + *psēn,* to scrape.]

Parchment—goat- or sheepskin—was expensive; monks copying texts by hand reused old sheets by scraping off the top layer (destroying in the process priceless classical texts that the Church condemned as pagan). Words written on the incompletely scraped earlier layers showed through.

The bound edition of my dictionary reveals deeper layers under the word "palimpsest" itself. After a bracketed history of the word's origin in earlier languages it adds, "See k^{w}*el-*[1] in Appendix." The Appendix in question lists Indo-European roots, the reconstructed basic elements of words that are common to most European and Indian languages. "K^{W}*el-*" turns out to be an ancient root meaning "to revolve, move around, sojourn, dwell." It gave rise to modern English words as diverse as cultivate (and therefore culture), cyclone, collar (which encircles the neck), pulley, and palimpsest.

I'll say more later about these old meanings and roots. Here I simply want to remind you that words are complex objects, structured with multiple levels of meaning below (and above and around and behind) their formal definitions. Choosing words and arranging them in an order appropriate to your purpose is much of what writing is about. In this basic way, writing is different from reading—as different as laying down paint on flat canvas is from viewing what appears to be a painted three-dimensional scene. Writing is analogous to weaving: a weaver works a thin yarn laboriously back and forth, in and out of a preliminary structure, until a broad visual pattern appears. Or, better, think of mosaic tile. Sometimes when I'm writing history, fitting together piece after piece of documented fact to make a picture, I feel as if I'm on my back trying to glue up a copy of the Sistine Chapel in mosaic tile.

Readers rarely experience writing as strings of words arranged on the page, however (if they do, the writing is calling attention to itself, deliberately or inadvertently). If a text engages a reader, the writing becomes transparent and she enters the story as if through a window into a dream. Something similar but much less complex happens when you watch television: your brain organizes the pattern on the screen (which is only rows of phosphor dots selectively illuminated by an electron beam) into an image. An even better analogy to writing and reading is a computer program and its output, because the phosphor dots on a television screen are organized automatically by a light-sensitive machine, but a computer program has to be written by human programmers, and what they write bears little or no resemblance to what happens on your display screen when the program executes—you may get a list of numbers, or toasters may fly.

If writing is making, what exactly is it that you make when you write? Most elementally, you make marks on a page that code for language.

Your reader scans them, sees and sounds them into words in his head, and processes them for meaning. The meaning for which your reader processes your words takes many forms—ideas, feelings, people, scenes, activities—all richly interconnected. At some level all writing, even a business letter or a technical manual, tells a story, at minimum a story about the writer; if your reader enters into the story you are telling, the various forms your words evoke merge into a whole. Samuel Taylor Coleridge, the English poet, called this process of words making worlds "poetic faith," defining it famously as a "willing suspension of disbelief."

Computer technology offers a more familiar analogy perhaps than a religious concept such as faith. Virtual reality is a technology for tricking your senses into believing you're experiencing a projected illusion. Gloves with built-in actuators enable you to "feel" a simulated object; a helmet with a built-in sound system, computer screens, and head- and eye-tracking sensors make it seem as if you are looking around and moving within a projected space. Virtual reality is a powerful illusion, with remarkable possibilities. Biologists, for example, expect one day to use it to learn how biomolecules such as proteins assemble themselves by assembling virtual biomolecules and *feeling* the molecular forces that allow and forbid various arrangements. Imagination, an ancient human invention, is a virtual-reality process, with the disadvantage that everyone has to make up the virtual reality on his own. Writing is a recording system that allows imagination to share its virtual treasures. What do you make when you write? Writing makes virtual reality inside readers' heads.

If you dislike technology, or fear it, you may find these analogies unpleasant. Stick with poetic faith if you prefer. I bring up technological analogies not to discomfort you but to try to specify more clearly what writing is about and how it works. My senior high school English teacher believed that the way to communicate her love of literature was to praise literature with superlatives. "Oh, Shelley, he's so *wonderful!* The *ineffable transcendence* of his poetry!" Her enthusiasm was refreshing at first, but finally it was wearing, because her superlatives were essentially appeals to authority, not explanations of why Percy Bysshe Shelley's "Ode to the West Wind" was worth my time. If you want to write, you need to know what you're doing, not why writing is superior to other human activities (it's not). Presumably you already believe writing is worthwhile, or you wouldn't be reading this book.

Understanding writing as the production of virtual realities clarifies why taking care with craft is so important. There are at least as many elements to manipulate in writing, to get the reality right, as a movie crew has to deal with in shooting a film (in fact, there are many more): dialogue, plot, character development, makeup, lighting, sets, props, camera angles, and montage just for starters. (D. W. Griffith, the pioneering filmmaker, said he learned montage reading Charles Dickens.) Behind those theatrical and cinematographic elements you have to organize words in all their palimpsestal complexity, sentences, rhythm, and structure at every scale from phrase to sentence to paragraph to chapter to book. (Words and sentences are the machine language of writing, if you will; the elements that writing shares with theater and film are already part of the shell program you create.) And you're only one person, not a whole crew. That sounds like a discouraging burden to bear. It can be when you're not getting the results you want, but fortunately you don't have to create and control everything at once: writers generate multiple drafts of a text because they organize the elements of writing successively rather than simultaneously. Fortunately also, the inherent richness and complexity of the writing process makes it continually interesting, far more challenging to attempt and satisfying to achieve than chess or any other game. It's the deepest and most fulfilling work I know, with the possible exception of farming.

Controlling the mechanisms of language for precise effect serves not only to shape the reader's virtual-reality experience but also to avoid distracting her from its illusions. How easily distracted the reader is—how much care you must take—depends on what you're writing. Judging from the evidence of best-sellers, readers of genre fiction are tolerant of what any writing teacher worth his salt would call sloppy writing, so long as the writer pushes the right genre buttons. If the spies intrigue, if the romance blossoms, if the horrors haunt, devoted readers apparently don't notice the quality of the writer's prose or don't care. I know of at least one popular, best-selling genre author who carefully goes through his draft manuscripts and substitutes clichés for any original turns of phrase that may have crept in, because he doesn't want to distract his readers with unfamiliar words and images and because he's established a consistent (clichéd) authorial voice across his shelf of books that he knows his readers expect to hear. Literary critics, who tend to judge all writing by the same high standard, may groan at these facts of life; genre readers read on enthusiastically, and genre writers laugh all the way to the bank.

Up another literary side street, poets structure their writing so rigorously that only the short forms have survived, with scant readership. The problem isn't that modern poetry is obscure, although sometimes it is; rather, the best modern poetry is so dense with fresh (and therefore unfamiliar) language that it's extremely demanding to read. Most of us aren't trained to such rigors. Nor does poetry fit the system most busy readers have organized for themselves of factual reading for work and citizenship, and narrative fiction, usually genre, for entertainment. Poetry isn't necessarily fiction and it isn't necessarily fact and it's hard work to read, so it falls between the bedstands.

I don't mean to be constructing a hierarchy here. Poets, with the defensiveness typical of embattled minorities, like to think prose is failed poetry written by people who can't come up to the mark; writers of literary prose look down on genre writers; genre writers think literary writers and poets are quixotic or self-indulgent. The truth is, each is writing in a different form, which has different requirements and meets different needs. James Joyce once claimed he could have written a stack of best-sellers in the time it took him to write *Ulysses.* He probably couldn't have written a popular novel if he tried; only rarely does a writer range successfully across that obscure divide. Music shows the same deep division between popular and classical, which suggests that it's a formal division, not the gulch between taste and tastelessness that high-culture critics hypothesize. Critics, like all consultants, have a vested interest in inflating the authority of their opinions.

The literary establishment would seem to consider technical writing beyond the pale (with rare exceptions, for example, literary prizes for science writing go to popularizations, not original scientific monographs), but I have read scientific papers of great power, power that derives not from rhetoric but from precision, logic, and originality of thought. Once you learn the necessary jargon of a particular branch of science, the classic papers of that science reveal themselves to be fully correlative to works of art. Robert Pollack, a molecular biologist, in his book *Signs of Life,* calls the 1953 *Nature* paper by James Watson and Francis Crick that announced their discovery of the structure and function of DNA "a nine-hundred-word prose poem," and he's right, it is.[1] Popular discussion of left-brain versus right-brain functions distorts the work of the neurobiologists and physicians Roger Sperry, Joseph Bogan, Michael Gazzaniga, and others, whose original papers, published in the journal *Brain* in 1965 and 1967, are "highly readable and well within the grasp of a high-school student," according to Sperry's fellow Nobel laureate David Hubel.[2] If I were teaching a writing course, I'd require my students to read scientific papers as well as other examples of exceptional prose; they're the best training I know in rigorous argument, a skill every writer can use.

It isn't possible in one small book to explore all the different requirements of all the different forms of writing (even if I knew and understood them, which I don't). The best way to do that in any case is to read and study the best texts of the form you wish to learn to write. But it's valuable to know—and most books about writing won't tell you—that different forms have different requirements. You'll save yourself a lot of confusion if you approach them without prejudice. I find I learn more by observing than by judging.

If you're interested in learning to write as well as you can, then the more forms you know, the better. The poet who scolded me about flacking for Hallmark should have told me I'd be better off *also* driving a cab; then I would have agreed with him. More experience with the forms of writing is better than less because forms set up expectations in readers, and knowing them helps you control your writing's effect. I don't mean you should practice by writing a spy novel, unless spy novels are what you want to learn to write, but it might be valuable to read one or two, along with poems, narratives, oral histories, novels, short stories, technical manuals, scientific papers, and any other printed matter that comes to hand. I subscribe to periodicals ranging from the distinguished British scientific journal *Nature* through the *New York Times* to the *National Enquirer*; each grants me treasures the others don't provide.

Writing isn't a zero-sum game. With fifty thousand books published every year in the United States alone, stacks of magazines and journals, reams of newspapers, newsletters, and other media, there's room for diversity. Civilization won't collapse if people write differently. Bad writing—writing that's irrelevant or incoherent—won't survive history's relentless winnowing. Many critics who disdain forms of writing they consider vulgar are simply intellectually provincial. Others cling to a romantic belief that writing is a kind of secular revelation. It may be, but the oracles speak through many different forms.

* * *

Software aside for the moment, back to hardware. Do you write with a word processor or do you write with a pencil? People almost always ask writers that question at public appearances. I used to wonder why. I couldn't understand why it mattered. But of course it does matter. How writers physically compose their work can seem to someone beginning to write to be a point of entry, another passage through fear. So I take the question seriously when I'm asked.

What equipment writers use to write depends on what's available and what they're comfortable with. Herman Melville wrote *Moby-Dick* with pen and ink on unlined paper. Everyone wrote that way in the centuries before mechanical writing machines. Along came the typewriter, which made manuscripts easier for typesetters to read but disconnected the writer from direct contact with the paper under her hand and the often tedious but sometimes sensual process of forming letters and words from a thin line of ink (a physical correlative to the linear writing process itself). Nor was it possible with the typewriter to see the whole page at one time and catch with peripheral vision the annoying repetitions that the dog drags in. Some writers still use manual typewriters today. The historian David McCullough, for one, clacks out his generous, thoughtful histories on an old office manual, demonstrating his great fortitude. E. J. Kahn, Jr., the *New Yorker* writer who died in 1994, wrote more than three million words across fifty-six years for that magazine on a mechanical Remington. "(He never yielded to the vogue for electric or electronic machines)," his anonymous *New Yorker* obituary notes in characteristically sniffy parenthesis. The magazine had the good sense to yield to the vogue, though, didn't it, unless it's still typeset by hand.

If you want to write only occasionally, stay with familiar equipment. But if you intend to write regularly, you'll almost certainly benefit from using a computer with a word-processing program. Computers adequate for word processing cost less than a thousand dollars new; used computers are cheap. The benefit of using a computer may not be obvious while you're learning the equipment and its quirks and limitations get in your way. The benefit comes when you begin revising a draft you've written, because revision is much easier electronically than it is on paper.

I learned to write writing love letters to a girl I'd met at church camp when I was fourteen. I was living at a home for boys by then. The girl was from another town. I couldn't travel to see her, so I wrote her. I wrote her four hundred letters in one year. I wrote with a ballpoint pen on school paper, and at 1.1 letters per day I must have done a lot of creative writing. I wish I'd kept the letters; I'd like to see what I had to say.

I took a typing course in high school. I had to convince the teacher to admit me to the class; typing in those days was considered secretarial and therefore, like home economics, exclusively for girls. (I argued that I needed the skill for college.) I wish I'd taken shorthand as well. When I got to college I bought a mechanical typewriter, a smooth Smith-Corona portable, and paid for it typing classmates' papers at five cents a page (ten cents if they wanted me to correct grammar and spelling, which they often did). I also learned to set type in college, pulling zinc letters smelling of machine oil out of a wooden type box to print headlines for the *Yale Daily News.* That experience, antique now, made language tangible. I dropped the zinc blocks one at a time upside down and backward into a steel type stick like a small version of the gadget shoe stores use to measure feet,* sometimes rewriting on the fly if the headline writer had miscalculated and the line was too long. Then I tightened the clamp on the type stick, set the stick into the bed of a proof press, inked the type with a black rubber roller (the ink snapping viscously as I rolled it smooth), laid a sheet of heavily

* A salesman at Brooks Brothers' New York store tells me the foot-measuring gadget is called a Brannock device—too obscure a name to throw into the sentence but useful to know. It's the only common object I can think of that looks anything like a type stick.

calendered white paper over the block, and pulled a proof to use for paste-up. While the proof was drying I wiped the leftover ink from the type and dismantled the words letter by letter back into the alphabet of the bins.

From a mechanical typewriter I progressed, many years later, to a bright-red IBM Selectric, the one with the clattering dervish ball, then to an electronic Olivetti, bulky as a copier, that had a one-line electronic display. For possible correction, the Olivetti held the line I was typing until I hit the carriage-return key, when, disconcertingly, it rat-a-tat-tatted the corrected line like a machine gun while I was trying to compose the next one.

I wrote *The Making of the Atomic Bomb* on the electronic Olivetti, with a sidekick Brother electronic portable for footnotes sheltering in its shade. That was the early 1980s, and the personal computer had just appeared, but I didn't think I could afford one and in any case believed learning to operate one would take too much time away from writing when I had deadlines to meet. The price I paid for that Luddite sentiment was retyping every chapter of my fifteen-hundred-page book manuscript at least ten times in the course of editing, which means I typed at least fifteen thousand pages. The time I wasted retyping would have seen me through computer school. After *The Making of the Atomic Bomb* was published, I bought a computer and a laser printer. Now I add new technology as it becomes available—most recently, a CD-ROM drive that puts a dictionary on-screen behind my word-processing program, where I can switch to it quickly when I need to look up a word.

To young people weaned on computers, this discussion must seem archaic. But equipment is important to writing, as it is to every craft. The problem most people have with adapting to new equipment is the awkward transition. Learning requires self-consciousness, and self-consciousness breaks the writing mood. I found the transition worth the temporary distraction. (It's certainly less distracting than quitting smoking.) With word-processing software, I edit more carefully now than I did before. Notebook computers make such software portable, but I rarely travel with a computer. I travel for research, which in my work results in either recorded tape (including my dictated notes) or copies of documents. I do my writing at home.

Back up everything you write, often. Not even the rigors of a colonoscopy match the pain of losing work and trying to reconstruct it from memory. Your memory dog will hide out in the break room, believe me, whimpering and listening to you rage.

I had never used a thesaurus until I tried the electronic version. I hadn't believed a generic compilation could improve on my own associative retrieval. It can't always, but it makes up for its lack of imagination with range. You can steer an electronic thesaurus around 180 degrees from wherever you begin simply by choosing the most remote synonym from each successive screen, and then steer it back around to your original word choice again along the same route. Somewhere among those 360 degrees of associated meanings is usually the word you're looking for or an association like a lost shoe that guides your dog straight to the fugitive. A dictionary entry is a good source of synonyms as well; the person who wrote the entry had to sort among synonyms to define the word. Before computers, I used to open a dictionary randomly when all else failed and plunge in. At minimum I learned a few new words or refreshed my knowledge of the meaning and history of words I thought I already knew. But often I found a fresh word that served my purpose. I wasn't usually searching for a synonym per se; I was usually looking for a word with overtones that matched whatever metaphor I was elaborating. That's still an incantation I have to do by hand. People lost in a wilderness have been known to find their way out guided by the wrong map; orienting is apparently a function only loosely tied to locality.

Checking spelling automatically is another computer convenience. My ability to spell hasn't rusted because I do; to the contrary, the checker has found words I used to misspell routinely and taught me how to spell them right.* Spelling checkers overlook a more subtle class of errors, however—words left embedded when you rewrite and delete and homonyms such as "thee" for "the." If you check your spelling automatically, you still need to proofread final manuscripts.

Electronic dictionaries save the heavy work of wrestling with a big hardbound dictionary. I'm looking forward to acquiring the CD-ROM version of the unabridged *Oxford English Dictionary,* the definitive English-language reference, because it's both exhaustive and strictly historical—twenty volumes searchable at the click of a mouse. Whether your dictionary is bound or electronic, use one that gives word histories, not merely definitions; all the music of words plays from their palimpsestal etymologies. Electronic dictionaries share a disadvantage of word-processing programs: you can't open them on your desk and see full pages side by side. Sometimes there's no substitute for laying out your work, looking it over in the large, and cutting and pasting, and for that you need hard copy. But once you've taped together a new sequence of text you can easily, if tediously, cut and paste its electronic counterpart, with the advantage that the electronic edges seamlessly reunite.

I print out my ongoing text from day to day and edit it in pencil. Around the time Truman Capote published *In Cold Blood,* I read somewhere that he always edited with Eberhard Faber (in 1965 Faber-Castell) Blackwing 602 soft lead pencils. Curious, I ordered a box and fell for their dark satin line and comfortable balance, and I use them exclusively for editing now. They smear if you try to erase, but when you're editing you don't need to erase; you simply strike through, making a palimpsest of rejected choices and leaving a trail of crumbs for your biographer.

Whatever equipment you use, it's difficult to write for more than

* I just checked this paragraph and found I'd mispelled (*sic*) "misspell."

four hours at a stretch. When I have a choice—when a deadline isn't pressing—I write in the morning and edit in the afternoon. I try to finish transcribing my hand editing back into my computer text the same day, so that I won't have to continue that mechanical work the next morning. Then the text is fresh in the morning, and so am I. Some writers I know would find my schedule burdensome. Others would find it featherweight—the prolific Joyce Carol Oates comes to mind.

A tape recorder is valuable for gathering information. If you transcribe your own interviews and notes, you'll be able to skip what's irrelevant; there are transcription machines available, with foot pedals and headsets, for any size recording tape. My wife, Ginger, who's a writer and radio journalist comfortable with recording machines, handles taping when I do interviews, allowing me to concentrate on the interview itself. We have the tapes professionally transcribed directly onto computer disks, after which Ginger usually checks the transcript against the tape and fills in any holes. After years of doing all that myself, I'm grateful for her help.

Bring home souvenirs, samples, photos, and videotape from your travels if you can. They help recreate the people and settings you want to write about. When I wrote *The Last Safari,* a novel set in East Africa, I projected slides of scenes I'd photographed onto the wall of my office to carry me back in memory to that extraordinary place.

We keep jars of pencils and three-by-five-inch cards in cardholders at hand everywhere in our house. Ideas come to you day and night when you're writing; a convenient stash of cards and pencils (Blackwing stubs accumulated from editing) makes it easy to write them down. The cards are small and sturdy enough to slip into a shirt pocket or to organize on a desktop without their blowing away. I have ten years of notes on three-by-fives toward a work of fiction I've been planning. It's a diligent mole; it seems to tunnel along tirelessly below consciousness, popping up at odd hours with treasures in its claws. For the first few years I simply threw the notes into a file. Then I happened to pull them out and read them. I was amazed at how many good ideas I'd accumulated. Worried that fire (or mildew in the okefenokee Connecticut woods where I live) might destroy them, I spent the next day typing them into a computer file. Now I add them to that file within a day or so of writing them but keep the originals as well, in a separate place.

In his final years, Henry James became so comfortable with the process of creation that he composed his novels and stories in his head and dictated them to a male secretary, who sat and typed what he heard. Though James's prose style had moved by then beyond its earlier baroque complexity to the ruffles and flourishes of rococo, the pages the secretary pulled from the typewriter needed hardly any editing at all.

What equipment you use for writing doesn't matter so long as it helps you write. On the other hand, I'd estimate that my computer, by automating routine work, has doubled my productivity, which compensates many times over for its steep initial learning curve. I'm looking forward to the day when its programming masters voice commands and I can dictate to it directly and watch the words roll out in line across the page like soldiers filing onto a parade ground for inspection.

Three

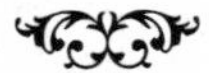

VOICES

The empty page is a Sphinx, blankly ferocious. I asked Ginger what was hardest about writing. She said, "All at once." At the beginning it is, a mortal riddle: whowhatwherewhenwhy? Gabriel García Márquez, the Colombian novelist and Nobel laureate, in the introduction to his short-story collection *Strange Pilgrims,* calls beginning "intense":

> Beginning a novel . . . everything must be defined in the first paragraph: structure, tone, style, rhythm, length, and sometimes even the personality of a character. All the rest is the pleasure of writing, the most intimate, solitary pleasure one can imagine, and if the rest of one's life is not spent correcting the novel, it is because the same iron rigor needed to begin the book is required to end it.[1]

As for the novel, so also, *mutatis mutandis,* for any work of writing: the first paragraph charts a course that may lead the reader—and will restrain the writer—through hundreds and even thousands of pages, to the near or distant end. And first among firsts is voice: who is telling the story?

Well, who *is* telling the story? You, of course. Only you. If it's a story about you or a story in which you participated or a story you observed, then it would seem that you could tell your story in your natural voice, whatever "natural" means, in the first person. But if you want to tell some other kind of story—a story you're making up, a story that happened last year or two hundred years ago that you're reconstructing from research, a newspaper story, a critical paper for school—who will tell the story then? Still you, but not you. Even the you who is telling your first-person personal story is you but not you, isn't it—is one but not another of your many persona, whichever one you've selected for this particular task? It follows that voice in writing—*who* is telling the story—is always to some degree made up for the occasion, which is to say, is always fictional, even when you intend to use that voice to convey documented fact.

Every work of writing, no matter how modest, no matter how seemingly "objective," no matter how "true," is composed in one or more fictional voices. "Someone" "tells" every story, even the copy on the back of cereal boxes, even a legal contract, even a street sign. We may not pause to puzzle out who "someone" is—the author may not even have thought about her choice of voice in advance—but we register "someone" 's presence and assess his statements accordingly. When I sit down to pay my monthly bills, I keep myself awake noticing all the different ways corporations have found to encourage me also to pay the postage. In a little box in the upper-right-hand corner of the return envelope, one orders, "Put stamp here." Another demands, "Place stamp here." "Please affix letter rate first class postage here," one requests pedantically. "Post Office will not deliver without postage," another warns. I understand that there's a complex story behind these helpful little messages. What amuses me about them is their different voices; I can picture billing-department executives working out their various strategies for encouraging my compliance, putting (or placing or affixing) the stamp of their own personalities on these small, ephemeral documents. "A man cannot utter two or three sentences," observes Ralph Waldo Emerson, "without disclosing to intelligent ears precisely where he stands in life and thought. . . ."

Voice and its grammatical correlate, point of view, shape the frame through which your reader experiences your story. That necessary frame limits what your reader will know, of course. But its limitations cut both ways. The frame of voice limits what your reader will know *because it limits what you can tell him.*

Newspaper reporters, reputedly a tough-minded lot, tend to scoff at such explications. Most of the reporters I've known hardly give a thought to literary issues. They're reporting the facts, which are synonymous in their minds with the truth. They know there are other points of view and other truths, but for them, reportorial truth carries superior authority. Style, including voice, is something laid out in the newspaper's stylebook. If you deviate from house style, the procrustean rewrite editor will adjust your style to fit. This process can be revealing. In the *New York Times,* for example, everyone mentioned in a story receives a courtesy title. For men it's "Mr." unless (so far as I can tell) "Mr." is a physician; then his courtesy title is "Dr." So when I referred to the controversial physicist Edward Teller in a book review I wrote for the *Times,* the editor who rewrote my idiosyncratic prose into uniform *Times*style forced Dr. Teller to surrender his doctorate and become Mr. Teller. A trivial matter, certainly, but a matter that raises a corner on the *Times*'s urban, bourgeois scale of values. If Edward Teller wanted an honorific from the *New York Times,* he should have gone into medicine.

More revealing was a stylistic sinkhole collapse that struck a provincial newspaper, which I'll call the *Express,* several years ago when its style gurus decided that gentility required a *Times*-like "Mr." on second and subsequent references to men. The *Express* more than the *Times* reports gory capital crimes; it soon found itself, in the name of gentility, calling the likes of John Wayne Gacy "Mr. Gacy" while the police exhumed the dismal harvest of corpses from the stalls and cavities of Gacy's fetid house. The *Express* had a failure of nerve; abruptly "Mr." disappeared before the last names of accused criminals but remained in place for honest citizens. Whereupon an astute reader raised the reasonable objection that omitting courtesy titles only before the names of accused criminals was tantamount to prejudging their guilt, and didn't the Constitution say we are innocent until proven guilty in a court of law, etc., etc. The *Express* first guiltily reinstituted the "Mr.," but then law-'n'-order citizens protested in their turn: the accused were monsters, not human beings, how could the *Express* do them the courtesy, what about the rights of the victims, etc., etc. A long silence from the *Express* as (I imagine) its ethics committee pondered vital issues of constitutional right. Then a desperate solution: the full given name of accused criminals henceforth appeared not only on first mention but on second and subsequent mentions thereafter. "Volunteer clown John Wayne Gacy was indicted today on multiple counts of first-degree murder. John Wayne Gacy was bound over to trial.... 'I'm innocent,' said John Wayne Gacy." By changing the rule governing only one seemingly minor point of style, the new policy gave the *Express*'s crime coverage a new voice, frontier antique, like the formal, uncontracted speech that cowboys speak in latter-day Hollywood westerns. The *Express* lost its footing on this particular banana peel in an attempt at gentility. The *Times,* more self-confident or perhaps more worldly, simply calls accused criminals "Mr.," like the rest of the folks.

Who is telling a newspaper story? Through their stylebooks and their rewrite desks, newspapers have organized a corporate voice, the fictional voice of a fictional observer who arrived on the scene after the deed was done and has to reconstruct it by asking people what they saw. As is always true with voices in writing, the characteristics that define the corporate newspaper voice as a voice, as a persona, also limit what it can say. If it seems to speak in violation of its "character," then that character becomes suspect or dissolves. (Consider, for example, the accusations by conservatives that the press has a "liberal" bias. Conservatives deduce such bias from their translation of the corporate newspaper voice, which they "hear" in their newspaper's choice of stories, choice of experts to comment within stories, "slant." They don't believe it's what it represents itself to be, a neutral observer.) So the newspaper voice can report what someone told it; it cannot report what it thinks about what it was told (that different voice is reserved for editorials, columns, and "opinion pieces"). It prefers oral statements to written documents, as if truth were better ascertained eye-to-eye; if Dr. Jones has announced a cure for cancer in the *New England Journal of Medicine,* a reporter will call him and ask him questions intended to elicit verbal statements similar to those that appear in Dr. Jones's report. Why not quote the report itself? I have no idea.

Since the newspaper voice is defined as having no opinions (even though the editors' value judgments are made abundantly evident by their choice, placement, and display of stories), reporters have to resort to a subterfuge to assess the validity of the information they gather: they report further statements gathered from other sources who are presumed to be knowledgeable on the subject in question. (Writers using the first-person-singular point of view—I—have a similar technical problem, which I'll discuss later in this chapter.) Editors decide which sources are credible. The bunker mentality of the Cold War, for example, led American newspaper editors to judge any source affiliated with the peace movement not to be credible, isolating that segment of the political spectrum, which received far more coverage in Europe. The same censorship on a smaller scale limited the press access of opponents of the war in Vietnam.

Obviously the rigid and wholly artificial—fictional—structure of the newspaper has consequences for the range and accuracy of the news we receive. I can easily imagine a newspaper made up of extracts from documents, interviews, congressional and courtroom testimony, books, medical and scientific papers, and other primary sources, each framed with succinct contextual explanation. Such a publication doesn't exist in America or anywhere else as far as I know, but the amusing and revealing Readings section of *Harper's* magazine demonstrates the potential of the form. All selection distorts, of course, so my *Daily Reader* would not be unbiased, but at least its subscribers would catch a glimpse of a primary source now and then. I suspect that the egalitarian clamor of such a publication would seem uncomfortably chaotic to most editors. Apparently editors, if not readers, prefer their news to be reported monolithically, a preference justified by a fiction of objectivity. The vehicle of that fiction is voice.

Many books on writing offer sets of rules similar to the rules in a newspaper stylebook, which define, wittingly or unwittingly, a standard expository voice. *The Elements of Style,* by William Strunk, Jr., with revisions and additions by E. B. White, the *New Yorker* essayist, is the best-known such book in the United States, a guide to what White in a concluding chapter calls "good standard English."[2] It's a useful compendium, but nowhere in the book does either Strunk or White mention voice and point of view. One consequence of this omission is that White finds nothing more helpful to say on the subject to the aspiring writer than "place yourself in the background" and "write in a way that comes easily and naturally to you."[3] It's useful to review such books of rules. As White says, "writing good standard English is no cinch," and knowing the good, standard rules can guide you.[4] At another level, though, style rules reveal the biases of those who formulate them; they define only one among many possible voices and styles. The Strunk and White voice—good standard English—is the voice of academic discourse, the voice in which most college papers are expected to be written (reason enough to learn it if you're attending college or college-bound), the voice of scholarly articles and books, those at least not strangled with jargon. It's actually an English voice more than an American, descended from the prose style favored by Victorian and Edwardian historians at Oxford and Cambridge. It's supposed to be a spare, cool voice, rational rather than emotional, but since reason and emotion come inextricably bound together in people and in words, it often sounds simply inhibited. White advises you not to use the language of advertising in your writing, for example, "for it is the language of mutilation." That's not a reason, that's a prejudice. Better advice might be to use words borrowed from advertising only knowingly and deliberately, as you should use every word you commit to the page when you write.

Good standard English is a valuable all-purpose tool to add to your kit; it slices and dices and even does the laundry. But you should understand that it is one voice among many, deceptively "objective" and not as rational as it pretends. I've read good standard analyses of how many millions of Soviet Russian citizens a particular U.S. plan of nuclear assault was expected to kill; I have no doubt the same horrors were bruited in good standard Russian as well.

Most books that purport to teach writing advise you to write as simply as possible. You may be constrained by a formal requirement, as students usually are in papers, in which case it's wise to comply. But good standard English isn't more virtuous than any other style. Painters don't paint only in black and white. Different voices, different styles, suit different purposes. The more of them you learn to command, the more resources you bring to writing.

Certainly every writer evolves a characteristic style—a way that comes easy to him, an idiosyncratic pattern of rhythm, word choice, and sentence structure as unique as a fingerprint. Literary detectives have even developed computer programs that analyze such regularities to identify patches of plagiarism in other writers' works. I'm so used to my own style after more than thirty years of professional writing that I find it difficult to copy out quotations without making typing errors—my fingers stumble because the rhythms of the text I'm copying aren't my own. But there's no such thing as a "natural" voice in writing. Do you have a natural speaking voice? In pitch, perhaps, although most people's speaking voices change pitch at times of tension—is such a changed voice then "unnatural"? Is a trained voice unnatural? ("Natural" is a hopeless word; it has always meant and continues to mean whatever the speaker wants to exclude from discussion. Ernest Rutherford said that whenever he heard one of his students use the word "universe" he threw him out of the laboratory. I feel the same way about the meaningless word "natural.") More to the point of writing, almost everyone adjusts her vocabulary and level of diction to suit the social circumstances of speech. We talk one way to authority figures, another way to friends, another way to children, another way when we're happily intimate with a lover, yet another way when we're angry (when we're angry we sound legal, as if we've already taken the case to court: "I jest not"; "Upon whose authority do you speak?"). Judging from man-in-the-street interviews, most Americans have given up waving at the camera and learned to talk television talk, a curious patois resonant with authority but almost devoid of content. Every work of writing will require you to color your characteristic style—your "natural" voice—to suit the circumstances of your story.

Voice is the first and sometimes the hardest decision a writer makes. If you don't know who is telling the story you are writing, then you will find the writing difficult, if not impossible. When I sat down to write my Donner Party novel, I'd spent two years studying my subject. I'd read everything I could find about the Donner Party, including the diaries some of the members of the party kept. I'd read broadly in the literature of the pioneer West. With my wife and children I'd driven and in places walked the California Trail that the Donners followed. I'd visited Donner State Park at Donner Lake in the Sierras and paced off the distances between the ruins of what had been the Donner cabins. I'd developed a chronology for the expedition and organized the information I'd collected under its rubric of days. All the information I needed was at hand, assembled in a big notebook; now I had to tell the story.

The Donner Party came together at Fort Laramie, in what would later be eastern Wyoming, from different tributary streams of emigrants. When the party reached the Sierra Nevada and encamped, the story would divide between the camp at the lake, another camp, a few miles downriver, and the rescue effort that developed over the mountains in California. The problem I had to solve, then, was finding a voice that could know simultaneously what was going on in all these different places but could also, because I wanted to get inside the emigrants' heads, shift imperceptibly into individual internal monologue to report people's thoughts. I also needed a voice that would not sound modern and therefore anachronistic.

I first tried the conventional voice of an omniscient narrator, third person and past tense. I drafted seventy-five pages that way, moving the emigrants from their homes in Illinois and Missouri through their organization into wagon trains in Independence, Missouri, out onto the prairie, green with spring grass. The voice never seemed to work. I felt as if I were writing with an opera storming in the background. The orchestration was wrong. It felt even *morally* wrong to tell the Donners' terrible, marvelous story of suffering and courage in God's or James Michener's unsuffering voice from on high.

I was quickly desperate. I had set aside six weeks to write this novel, all the time that I could afford to take off from earning a living as a magazine writer. I calculated I needed twelve pages a day to finish in six weeks, and I was already seventy-five pages behind. What should I do? I poked around among the books I had on hand for reference, looking for a hint of a voice I could adapt. I kept coming back to one book, the diary of a remarkable mountain man named James Clyman. Clyman, coming east from California in the summer of

1846, had encountered the Donners going west and had warned them not to take a trail cutoff he had just traversed, which they believed would save them time. They rejected his advice, a rejection that sealed their fate. They'd read about Hastings' Cutoff in a book and trusted the book more than Clyman, who in their eyes was only a trapper in greasy buckskins. He was in fact a paragon of sensibility and of survival lore and a clear, authentic, contemporary voice:

> [July] 15 This stream affords some rich vallies of cultivateable land and the Bluffs are made of a fine lime rock with some good timber and numerous springs of clear cool water here I observed the grave of Mrs. Sarah Keyes agead 70 yares who had departed this life in may last at her feet stands the stone that gives us this information This stone shews us that all ages and all sects are found to undertake this long tedious and even dangerous Journy for some unknown object never to be realized even by those the most fortunate and why because the human mind can never be satisfied never at rest allways on the strech for something new some strange novelty[5]

Clyman's was the voice I needed; I only had to go one step further and use it omnisciently. It could slip into the minds of the Donner emigrants without jarring the reader's ear. It could stand back and look down at the rescuers toiling up the western Sierra slope, the desperate groups trying to descend from the mountains through the deep, deadly snow, the families hunkered down in their snow-buried cabins east of the frozen lake, and it would not seem omniscient so much as retrospective, like a man telling the tale to the next summer's emigrants around a campfire. In fact, having chosen to adapt Clyman's voice, I decided to write my novel as a fictional diary, one entry for every day of the year-long journey, and it worked:

December 22
With no food in camp except the bear meat hidden in Eddy's pack the Forlorn Hope set out at dawn following the only trail they knew down the stream canyon south. Over the ridge behind them lay Bear Valley and the food Reed and McCutchen had cached in Jothan Curtis's wagon but only Stanton could have found the trail. He had not come up during the night and they feared the worst for him. They debated going back to find him but with their food gone they knew they would only put themselves in worse danger. They drank hot water to stay their bellies and stumbled on. They hadn't traveled a mile when a storm broke from menacing low clouds swirling across the mountains beyond the canyon. The clouds came on and closed overhead and in minutes they could see no more than the canyon itself. They shouted up and down the line to halt and came together at an outcropping of rock that partly blocked the wind. They couldn't go on in the storm. They were too weak to fight the wind while they fought the snow. Eddy and the Indians moved out from the protection of the rock and began cutting wood. Breaking off branches to feed a fire. The women came out and dragged the wood back. They said Stanton might still come up but Mary Graves knew otherwise. Stanton had left them for a better place. Hell itself would be a better place. They were already half out of their minds with hunger.[6]

I finished the novel in the six weeks I had allotted myself. At 370 pages, it's the best of the four novels I've published so far.

Choosing which voice you will use to tell a story is not, then, an entirely arbitrary decision. To the contrary, voice is the first of many solutions you will have to find to the problem of answering the mortal riddle of the blank page. As I discovered writing *The Ungodly*, the right voice will carry the story; the wrong voice will weight it down or stall it entirely. Find the right voice, I tell students, and the story will tell itself. It's not that easy, of course, but the right voice at least allows the story to be told.

Voice really is almost as obscure as character in writing. Where does the voice come from that you find to tell a story? I didn't only borrow Clyman's voice. I also heard it in my head. My father was a Missouri farm boy with a third-grade education; my mother was born in a log cabin in Arkansas. The boys' home where I lived for six years during adolescence was a working farm. I knew the midwestern dialect that Clyman and my antecedents spoke and knew the kind of people who spoke it. I'd done a good job of damaging my ear for it at Yale, where I'd taught myself to speak an affected British English as an ill-conceived social disguise. I could still recover it on the page.

But something more than mimicry was involved. Besides being technically right, voice also has to be psychologically right for you if it's going to work, if you're going to be able to sustain it across the length of a book. Sustaining a consistent voice across the length of a work of writing—weeks, months, even years—is an emotional challenge as well as a technical problem. When I wrote *The Ungodly* I was still a young man looking for benevolent father figures to substitute for the father who had not protected me from abuse and who had abandoned me to the boys' home when I was twelve. James Clyman, the wise, resourceful mountain man, was such a benevolent figure. By putting on his voice, so to speak, I could put on his benevolence; I could be the good father to the Donner story that my father had failed to be for me. I could find and recreate imaginatively what was redemptive in the story, a story most people dismiss as disgusting because the emigrants survived by eating their dead. The emigrants went to such seeming extremity heroically, *to save their children*—that's what I found redemptive in the Donner story.

"Storytelling is fundamental to the human search for meaning," writes Mary Catherine Bateson in *Composing a Life*.[7] Why do you suppose you want to write, to tell stories? For others, of course, for fun, for glory, for the game and the endlessly fascinating puzzle of it, but also always to rewrite and restage your own inner dramas. Any serious writer who denies that aspect of her work is lying to herself. True works of art happen, I suspect, only when inner and outer come together. That's an important reason they're so rare. William Faulkner, who published more than twenty books, used to say that there were one-book writers, two-book writers, and, rarely, three- and four-book writers—meaning books that became classics and lived on. He thought he was a two-book writer at best or maybe a three-. But then he credited Ernest Hemingway and F. Scott Fitzgerald with only one each. God knows one ought to be gift enough for anyone.

Point of view is easier. There aren't that many choices: first person, indirect first person, second person, third person, present tense, past tense.

The best-known American first-person fiction is probably *Moby-Dick*, with its forthright opening sentence, "Call me Ishmael."[8] Herman Melville had technical problems with Ishmael's voice as he went along, however; its limitations of range led him to cast several chapters as dramatic scenes in play form, and once he required Ishmael to quote himself telling a story at length in "the style in which I once narrated it at Lima."[9]

First person, past tense is a good way for beginning writers to tell a story. As voices go, it's straightforward, its boundaries reasonably clear. It's a familiar voice; we normally frame the ongoing narrative of our lives in the first person, past tense. "Where were you?" "I was out walking the dog and I stopped to buy an ice cream cone." But a first-person narrator must be a participant in the story he's telling, and his involvement limits his information. He can report only what his senses reveal, what others tell him, what he knows, and what he speculates. I deliberately chose an informal voice and the first-person, past-tense point of view for this book because I wanted to feel, and I wanted you to feel, as if I were speaking to you personally, passing along what I've learned about writing. (I chose to address the reader as "you" rather than the more formal "one," "he/she," or "the reader," for the same reason.)

First person, present tense is a stylish new point of view borrowed from the screenplay: "I'm out walking the dog and I stop to buy an ice cream cone. My sister Susan is there eating peppermint stick, her favorite flavor." To my old-fashioned ear it sounds distinctly odd, and I don't see its advantages, but who am I to say?

For my second novel, *Holy Secrets,* I planned to write about the shattering of a marriage, a personal story that the central character, a man who's a gynecological surgeon, would narrate. I had just been through the shattering of a marriage myself, however, and felt uncomfortable with first-person narration; I found it difficult to disentangle my personal "I" from the fictional "I" I was attempting to create (and of course the story contained autobiographical elements, which made the dissonance worse). I settled instead on a more comfortable alternative, indirect first person—first person cast as third person, past tense—as in the novel's opening paragraph:

> Lost in the middle of life, he was a surgeon and he knew what people said of surgeons: that they liked to cut. Through the window between the scrub room and the operating room Tom Haldane watched Rena prep Mrs. Corso, the long sponge for-

> ceps dripping Phisohex onto the nude and wrinkled abdomen and plunging below. The anesthetist bent among his tanks and tubes, a scuba instructor at the deck of the green pool, already conducting the woman's breathing, pumping the black bag, contemptuously sponsoring her relief. Having learned his trade in the Air Force on the Vietnamese, the anesthetist didn't believe in pain.[10]

(That's four characters introduced in the first paragraph and an allusion to Dante's *Divine Comedy;* not bad.)

Indirect first person positions a narrative somewhere between the narrow egocentricity of first person with its "I"s and "me"s and the enlarging historical authority of third person. As a point of view, it's limited precisely as direct first person is limited, yet it feels to the writer (and perhaps to the reader as well) a little more spacious.

Indirect first person is also the point of view writers use when they want to fit internal monologue into third-person narrative. In the selection from *The Ungodly* I quoted earlier, the point of view shifts smoothly from third to indirect first person to record Mary Graves's thoughts (a shift I'll indicate here with italics): "The women came out and dragged the wood back. They said Stanton might still come up *but Mary Graves knew otherwise. Stanton had left them for a better place. Hell itself would be a better place. They were already half out of their minds with hunger.*"

The past tense of past-tense narrative is past perfect: "Stanton had left them" rather than, if he were present in the narrative past of the story, "Stanton left them" (present as the women are present who "came out and dragged the wood back"). The past perfect quickly calls attention to itself; it begins to sound stilted if it's carried on too long. Sometimes you can quietly shift back from past perfect to past after you've established that you're referring to past events, then shift again to past perfect when you're through. That's what I did in this paragraph from my narrative history *The Making of the Atomic Bomb,* which looks back on the earlier life of the Hungarian physicist and visionary Leo Szilard from the vantage point of 1933:

> In 1928, in Berlin, where he was a *Privatdozent* at the University of Berlin and a confidant and partner in practical invention of Albert Einstein, Szilard had read [H. G.] Wells's tract *The Open Conspiracy.* The Open Conspiracy was to be a public collusion of science-minded industrialists and financiers to establish a world republic. Thus to save the world. Szilard appropriated Wells's term and used it off and on for the rest of his life. More to the point, he traveled to London in 1929 to meet Wells and bid for the Central European rights to his books. Given Szilard's ambition he would certainly have discussed much more than publishing rights. But the meeting prompted no immediate further connection. He had not yet encountered the most appealing orphan among Wells's Dickensian crowd of tales.[11]

Formally, "had read Wells's tract" should have been followed by "Szilard *had* appropriated," "*had* used," "he *had* traveled," "the meeting *had* prompted." In the interests of simplicity, but also to imbue the past (past perfect) events with present (past) immediacy, I shifted the tense. I make these adjustments by ear. You want your reader emphatically *not* to notice them but simply to be carried on by the narrative.

Second person, present tense isn't much used: "You walk out the door, climb on your bicycle, and ride down the street. You're sorry for what you just said to him. . . ." Second person, past tense is even rarer: "You walked out the door, climbed on your bicycle, and rode down the street. You were sorry . . ." "You," if it refers to the reader, risks confusion, since what you seem to be asserting about the

reader may conflict with the reader's own experience of himself. The second person turns up in writing usually as dialogue, more rarely as a kind of internal monologue: "You walked out on me. You didn't even say you were sorry. . . ." I use second person in this book to mean you, the reader, but also sometimes to mean me. Since we're both involved together here in thinking about writing, the unusual point of view seemed justified.

Voice and point of view are the most important but not the only challenges you have to meet in the first paragraph of a story. García Márquez mentions "structure, tone, style, rhythm, length, and sometimes even the personality of a character." You also have to decide where to begin your story; where to enter real or fictional history. Classically, there are two ways to begin a story: *ab ovo* and *in medias res. Ab ovo* means "from the egg"—from the beginning. *In medias res* means "in the middle of things"—in the middle of the action. Very few modern books begin *ab ovo.* Writers and their editors assume, probably correctly, that modern readers want to know immediately if a book will engage their attention. When I helped Luis Alvarez organize his memoir, *Alvarez,* I moved his chapter on flying the Hiroshima atomic-bombing mission from the middle of the book to the beginning, estimating that such a momentous experience would catch a potential reader's attention more immediately than Luie's reconstruction of the wanderings of his paternal grandfather. Luie had begun his narrative *ab ovo;* I grafted onto that beginning a prologue *in medias res.* Laurence Sterne played with these two approaches to beginning a book two centuries ago in his wonderful comedy *Tristram Shandy.* He began the book at its narrator's conception ("I wish either my father or my mother, or indeed both of them, as they were in duty both equally bound to it, had minded what they were about when they begot me"), literally *ab ovo,* but then had marbleized endpapers bound into the center of the book so that a reader who preferred to begin *in medias res* could adjust *Tristram Shandy* accordingly simply by opening

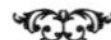

to the middle of the book and bending the front and back around 180 degrees so that the endpapers take their customary place on the outside.

The prologue technique that I suggested to Luie is commonplace these days. I tend to resist it in selecting books to read, feeling a little as if I'm being tricked. Writing is full of tricks, of course, but some tricks are more clever and even more profound than others; I couldn't rewrite Luie's memoirs to punch up his beginning, since they weren't mine to rewrite, so I had to rearrange. With *The Making of the Atomic Bomb* I used another technique, tying a knot in time. I began the book at a moment in 1933 important to the story of the discovery and development of nuclear energy, went backward from that point to review Leo Szilard's earlier life, then returned to the 1933 event and finished describing it. Thus Chapter One. Chapter Two then retreats to 1895, to an important earlier event, and only after carrying the history of physics forward to the 1933 event—on page 195—does the narrative pick up where it left off at the end of Chapter One.

Since I know what I was about when I wrote it, let me reproduce the first paragraph of *The Making of the Atomic Bomb* here so we'll have an opening paragraph we can discuss:

> In London, where Southampton Row passes Russell Square, across from the British Museum in Bloomsbury, Leo Szilard waited irritably one gray Depression morning for the stoplight to change. A trace of rain had fallen during the night; Tuesday, September 12, 1933, dawned cool, humid and dull. Drizzling rain would begin again in early afternoon. When Szilard told the story later he never mentioned his destination that morning. He may have had none; he often walked to think. In any case another destination intervened. The stoplight changed to green. Szilard stepped off the curb. As he crossed the street time

cracked open before him and he saw a way to the future, death into the world and all our woe, the shape of things to come.[12]

The first thing that must be obvious is that I don't explain who Leo Szilard is. I tried to work in his identification, but after much struggle concluded there wasn't room. I trusted the reader to assume that he must be related to the atomic bomb in some way, since that was the announced subject of the book. The second paragraph begins "Leo Szilard, the Hungarian theoretical physicist," so I kept the reader waiting only half a page.

I knew the book I was starting to write would be a long book, although I never imagined it would finish out at nearly nine hundred pages. I had come to think of the story I was about to tell, which I had researched exhaustively for six years, as the tragic epic of the twentieth century. Its theme, worthy of Milton, was "Humankind invents the means of its own destruction." I needed a narrative voice that could tell such a story with authority (more authority than I felt personally, since I had only one college physics course to my name). Such a voice was available in the Anglo-American tradition of historical narrative, in which I had been schooled as a history major; Edward Gibbon used it most notably for his *Decline and Fall of the Roman Empire.* I wanted to avail myself of that tradition but warm it up. To warm my narrative was largely a matter of deciding to tell the story as a group biography of the several hundred extraordinary human beings who caused it to happen. Then I found that I could keep a formal tone by the simple device of never using contractions. The only contractions that appear in *The Making of the Atomic Bomb* appear within quotations. "Was not" never becomes "wasn't." To warm the historical voice also meant incorporating vivid detail and borrowing devices from fiction. In particular, I saw that I could organize details in such a way that the reader used to the conventions of modern fiction might choose to read them as a historical personage's internal monologue.

All the details in the opening paragraph are accurate. Szilard left a taped oral history describing his irritation that morning at an article he had read while sitting in the lobby of the Russell Hotel. He said he threw down the paper and went out walking. I found the weather for the morning of September 12, 1933, in the London *Times,* on microfilm at a university library. The last sentence in the paragraph is editorial comment, so to speak, but the tradition of historical narrative allows room for such comment. Szilard had an idea as he crossed the street for what he called a "chain reaction," the basic energy-producing mechanism of nuclear reactors and atomic bombs. "Time cracked open before him and he saw a way to the future" seemed to me a reasonable metaphoric description of so pivotal an insight. Since I was writing a tragic epic about humankind inventing the means of its own destruction, evoking *Paradise Lost*—"death into the world and all our woe"—seemed appropriate. "The shape of things to come," as I revealed on the next page of the chapter, was the title of an H. G. Wells novel, reviewed in the *Times* twelve days before Szilard's walk, which concerned the state of the world after a destructive nuclear war—something futuristic, I thought, to set against the antique invocation of Milton. (It was also a private reference. *The Shape of Things to Come* was made into an Alexander Korda movie starring Raymond Massey, which had deeply impressed me when I saw it as a child. It had probably set me on the course that led me to write a history of the discovery and application of nuclear energy. Closing the circle, my editor for *The Making of the Atomic Bomb* was Alexander Korda's nephew Michael.)

I could have started so complex a story almost anywhere; but a man stepping off a curb is a human and engaging place to begin. (All stories are ultimately the same story: someone falls into a hole and has to find a way to get out.) For the first fifteen or twenty drafts of the opening paragraph, as I recall, the paragraph began with the words "Leo Szilard." But "Leo Szilard waited irritably one morning at a corner of Southampton Row in London for the stoplight to change" was clumsy. Worse, Szilard never mentioned what the cross street was. Shifting the geographical information to the front of the sentence, which I managed during the next fifteen or twenty drafts of the paragraph, suspended the reader in a place, a somewhat exotic place for American readers ("Bloomsbury," the district where Szilard was walking, evoked the Bloomsbury Group, an evocation that had nothing whatsoever to do with the story but added to the period flavor of the description). The sentence next introduced Szilard, then described what he was doing—but even that much was suspended, a cascade of suspensions. I had not yet identified Szilard beyond his unusual name; he was waiting for a stoplight, but where was he going when the stoplight changed? At the same time, by shifting the geographical information up front I was able to finesse the unidentified street corner and just have Szilard waiting "in London" somewhere along Southampton Row—all I reliably knew about his location.

Once I've established that a man is waiting at a stoplight, shifting to a description of the weather and his state of mind evokes for the literate reader the shift from third person to indirect first person that I discussed earlier in this chapter. Professional historians may complain that such an arrangement violates their rules of "objectivity." I've seen *The Making of the Atomic Bomb* described dismissively as "docudrama." I don't agree. I made up nothing in the book except its arrangement of the facts, as my fifty-six pages of careful footnotes confirm. What is fictional is what is fictional in all narrative, including the articles historians write that some imagine to be objectively "true": the voice in which the story is told and the arrangement of the information.

I hope that this detailed exegesis has been useful. At minimum it should demonstrate the extent to which writing is a process not of inspired free association but of concrete problem solving. Inspiration, if you will, comes out of the process of problem solving, not the other way around. In a 1987 interview, the ceramics designer Eva Zeisel described the process in the context of industrial design:

> I came to the conclusion that what we call limits—yes, industrial design is very limiting—was just the opposite; it was very unlimiting. I set my students this project. I said, "Please sit down and do the most beautiful thing you can imagine. You must have been thinking a lot about it." And they were sitting around totally frustrated, without the slightest idea of how to fulfill their dream. Then I gave them limitations—"Make something this high, with this function"—and suddenly they were all sitting there working like beavers.[13]

The most beautiful thing you can imagine will never leave your head, because it doesn't have a voice, or it has too many voices, and when you write it down you will have to invent a voice or to choose. The story that emerges will be far from the beautiful thing you imagined, but it will be at least a part of your ideal, one view, and it will be real, an object you crafted into existence, out on the paper where you can share it. Put it away for a while and come back to it, reread it, and you'll ask yourself with awe, "Who wrote that?"

Four

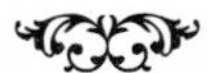

RESEARCH

I've never liked the word "nonfiction." "Non-Christian" hardly encompasses all the rich and various traditions of Judaism, Islam, Confucianism, Shinto, Hinduism, and the many other religions of the world, and "nonfiction" hardly does justice to the many kinds of writing it lumps together. It's derivative from "fiction," with no long history; the first reference the *Oxford English Dictionary* cites dates from only 1909. It defines a major category of human endeavor—encompassing essays, historical narrative, contemporary narrative, autobiography, biography, and reportage—with an empty negative. I've proposed a more descriptive technical term to refer to the literature of fact: "verity," pronounced like "clarity," from the Latin *veritas,* "truth." From here on I'll use that term to distinguish fiction from its factual counterpart and speak of fiction and verity. If "verity" sounds odd to you, new coinages usually do. It quickly becomes comfortable.

Considered as a craft, technically, the writing of fiction and the writing of verity are identical processes but for one significant difference: we expect the information conveyed in verity to conform to verifiable external references, while the information conveyed in fiction need be only internally consistent. This statement frequently shocks fiction writers. They're used to thinking of their work as wholly dif-

ferent from verity, invented rather than reported. If they're honest they'll usually admit that they think fiction aesthetically superior as well, drawing on deep sources of creative invention they suppose not to be available to the veritist, who they presume merely reports mundane fact. Especially if they write fiction improvisationally, coming fresh to a story every morning and playing it out by its own emerging rules, they see no such parallel process in verity. There is such a process, of course; it's called writing an essay, and it is, or can be, equally as improvisational as its fictional counterpart.

But there's a deeper sense than the technical in which the two kinds of writing, fiction and verity, are closer than we like to acknowledge: facts are always only provisional, subject to further verification and revision. Facts are constructed, in verity as in other forms of discourse, and their authority is based on conventions to which a greater or lesser number of people voluntarily agree. Readers assess works of verity by rules of credibility and internal consistency similar to the implicit rules they use to assess works of fiction; in the case of works of verity, however, they expect confirmation from external references as well. It was a "fact" in the southern United States two hundred years ago that the Holy Bible justified human slavery. Only within a particular framework of convention is it a "fact" that the earth revolves around the sun. From another and more intuitively obvious point of view, the sun revolves around the earth. Western science prefers the heliocentric perspective because it fits more efficiently within the larger framework of planetary and galactic astronomy, itself a reality constructed through the complex interpretation of data. I know such a statement is offensive to traditionalists. That doesn't relieve them of the responsibility of considering it.

I learned about facts on the first day of my first college course in historiography, which is the methodology of writing history. Louis P. Curtis, the historian who taught the course, proposed that we prove what every English schoolchild knows, that Charles I, king of England from 1625 to 1649, was beheaded during the English Civil War that brought Oliver Cromwell to power. Mr. Curtis gave each of us a document reference to look up and asked us to write a report on what we found.

My reference was a volume of the *Annals of Parliament* for 1649. I found an original edition, bound in parchment, in the open stacks at the Yale Library. Struggling with the antique typeface that used *f*'s for *s*'s, I skimmed through the volume. Eventually I found what I was looking for: a resolution approving the expenditure of some shillings for black paint to robe the executioner's scaffold.

The class reconvened. Everyone had discovered a fact that proved that the English people had beheaded their Scottish king. Mr. Curtis listened patiently to our reports. Then he summarily demolished them. An order for paint doesn't prove a beheading. A conviction of treason and a death sentence don't prove a beheading. Not even an eyewitness account proves a beheading. All might be misinformed or mistaken or fraudulent. History, Mr. Curtis shocked us by saying, is past, gone, unrecoverable in its authentic facticity, and the writing of history is necessarily provisional, a matter of sifting the limited evidence and deducing what is probable and plausible and what is not. No accumulation of documents proves anything in and of itself. Which was not to say there weren't standards of evidence on which responsible historians could agree. But not final proof. Never final proof. I understood Mr. Curtis's point well enough when I was twenty years old. I understand it even better now that I've wrestled with documents and written books of history myself. If you doubt it, think about the bizarre and ongoing debate concerning the assassination of John F. Kennedy.

Whatever the authority of facts, everyone does research to prepare for writing, even writers of fiction, even poets, even if the only library they consult is memory. You can't write without it. If writing is the construction of virtual realities, you have to get the reality right or the illusion falls apart. In the case of fiction, the reality may not be the "real" reality; it will still have to be consistent within itself and consistent with the real world wherever the two overlap. If you exchange Saint Basil's Cathedral and the Eiffel Tower in a story, you'll have to justify switching them between Moscow and Paris. A former editor of mine, a native New Yorker whose experience west of the Hudson River was as slight as that of most New Yorkers, wrote a novel some years ago that included a car chase through the cornfields of western Kansas. Since there aren't any cornfields in western Kansas—farmers there grow wheat; it's too dry for corn—I wondered how the editor came to be so fundamentally misinformed. Then it dawned on me. He'd taken his information from the musical *Oklahoma!*, where equally misinformed easterners cause ersatz farm folk to sing, "I'm as corny as Kansas in August. . . ." God's truth.

There are two basic kinds of research: document research and experience. Both are valuable; neither one is exclusive. You can sometimes arrange to experience even history. The B-29 that dropped an atomic bomb on Nagasaki is on display at the museum at Wright Patterson Air Force Base outside Dayton, Ohio. When I visited the museum in the course of researching *The Making of the Atomic Bomb*, the director allowed me onto the flight deck of *Bockscar* to try out the bombardier's seat. That experience helped me write knowledgeably about the bomb run. Paleontologists, by learning to flake spearpoints with tools like those that earlier species of *Homo* used, clarify the toolmaking process. The great benefit of experience is that your senses gather information directly and you feel it. No collection of documents is ever as rich in felt detail as experience itself. That's both a loss and a gain, writes the critic and biographer Lionel Trilling:

> Some of the charm of the past consists of the quiet—the great distracting buzz of implication has stopped and we are left only with what has been fully phrased and precisely stated. And part

> of the melancholy of the past comes from our knowledge that the huge, unrecorded hum and buzz of implication was once there and left no trace—we feel that because it is evanescent it is especially human. We feel, too, that the truth of the great preserved monuments of the past does not fully appear without it. From letters and diaries, from the remote, unconscious corners of the great works themselves, we try to guess what the sound of the multifarious implication was and what it meant.[1]

On the other hand, documents thoroughly studied can be remarkably revealing. Because James Clyman spelled phonetically, his diary discloses not only his words but also how he pronounced them. The independent scholar Chuck Hansen accumulated information sufficient to write a book about the development of American nuclear weapons by reading between the lines of tens of thousands of sanitized government documents. (Sanitizing means physically cutting classified information out of the documents with scissors.) Chuck discovered that different copies of the same document were often sanitized differently by different declassification officers; by comparing copies he could sometimes legally reconstruct deleted information, a process analogous to reading a palimpsest, which pointed to what government agencies considered most important in the documents—not only technical information but frequently also political information that the agencies sought to suppress. Draft manuscripts with their deletions and amendments allow biographers to describe with authority the evolution of an author's ideas (editing on a computer screen means much of that information is now being lost). Just as it's possible for astronomers to extract from the seemingly limited, white, point-source light of a star a range of information about the star's size, color, temperature, age, and companions, so also is it possible to extract much more information from documents than simply their manifest content.

Doing so is primarily a matter of paying attention, comparing one source of information with another, considering who wrote the document and why, and watching out for unusual details. In an early-twentieth-century popular novel I found the phrase "I was shaved" instead of "I shaved" and was reminded vividly that in those days men left their homes every morning for the male social forum of the barbershop (while women took care of their hair at home, a reversal of the present arrangement). Dwight Eisenhower's description of his horror when, home on leave from West Point in civilian clothes, he was casually identified by the operator of a firing range as a "soldier boy" helped me understand the extent to which he tried to mask his inner self from view even as a young man. A lecturer's use of the verb "to fish" in 1943 to designate the process of nuclear fission ("It would require about n = 80 generations . . . to fish the whole kilogram") gave me a measure of how new and unexplored was the discovery of how to release nuclear energy in the early days of the American atomic bomb project (scientists eventually settled on the verb "to fission").

The beginning of research is usually choosing a subject. That isn't necessarily as straightforward as it sounds. Many people feel a compelling desire to write before they know what they want to write about. How do you find a subject? One way is to start keeping notes and files. I have a file called "Futures," where I throw three-by-five notes of story ideas and newspaper clippings that suggest possibilities for both verity and fiction. When I identify a subject that interests me, I set up a file, read related articles and books as they come along, and file the notes my reading generates. For years I collected remaindered books and other documentary materials with the intention of someday writing a history of public health, for example. Public health measures are responsible for the dramatic decline across the past two centuries of epidemic disease, one of the great triumphs of our species. Recently, as a member of a foundation grant committee, I was able to direct support for that project to someone with far better credentials than I, a knowledgeable, experienced research physician. So I've closed, a little wistfully, that particular file. But it's one among many; I have more than enough subjects marinating in my files and in my head to occupy me with writing for the rest of my life.

Writers don't always work from a life list, however. Sometimes subjects appear in the sky like novas and demand to be observed. I was well along in research toward a straightforward history of the development of the hydrogen bomb when the demise of the Soviet Union made available for the first time documents that outlined the remarkable story of Soviet nuclear weapons development. Adding that story to *Dark Sun* delayed the completion of that book by two years, but it was too important a story to ignore, especially since the Soviet success in producing an atomic bomb motivated the United States to accelerate its hydrogen bomb effort.

Choosing a subject with which you may have to live for years is serious business. Before he began researching his best-selling biography of Harry S. Truman, David McCullough contracted with his publisher to write a biography of Pablo Picasso. Four months of looking into Picasso's undomesticated life convinced David that he couldn't stand the man. He then had to extricate himself from his contractual agreement to write a Picasso biography. Fortunately, he and his publisher were able quickly to agree on a biography of Truman, whom McCullough admired. Arianna Stassinopoulos Huffington took over the Picasso project. She couldn't stand Picasso either, but she turned her loathing into a successful hostile biography.

At the boys' home where I grew up, the Andrew Drumm Institute, a sturdy, generous man named George Berkemeier taught vocational agriculture and supervised our farmwork. George became Drumm Institute superintendent after I graduated. When he retired, he decided to write a biography of Andrew Drumm so that the founder's interesting story wouldn't be lost. Drumm, a pioneer midwestern cattleman who supplied meat to the miners of the 1849 California gold rush and ranched in Oklahoma's Cherokee Strip, accumulated a considerable estate, which he left to endow the farm school that still bears his name. George had discovered what many writers discover when they go to the library to look up the definitive reference on a subject that interests them—that there isn't one. No one has written that book yet, or someone wrote such a book long ago that's out of date by now, or there are ten books on the subject and none of them is worth a damn. So George Berkemeier, a retired schoolteacher and administrator in his seventies, went off to the local historical society, exhumed the story of Andrew Drumm, wrote a definitive biography, published it himself, and sold and gave away several hundred copies. I'm on the board of trustees of the Drumm Institute now; we're arranging to reprint George's book to use for fund-raising. We'll probably keep it in print for years to come.

My friend Bonnie Ruehter, partner with her husband, Jim, on a big cattle, hog, and grain farm in central Missouri, researches the Ruehter family tree when she can spare time from farming. Bonnie visits county courthouses and churches to track down the record of the family's genealogy across the United States and back to nineteenth-century Germany. She calls her hobby "family-treeing." She charts genealogies and writes up her research as she goes along in a notebook that she intends to pass along to her children. Informally, Bonnie is assembling the history of a family.

Barbara Hamilton, a small, careful, white-haired woman who contacted me after I published my autobiographical memoir, *A Hole in the World,* decided in her seventies to write a book about the destructive effects on her life of her childhood experience of incest. She was especially motivated to write when she understood through therapy that repressing her experience had led her passively to tolerate its destructive repetition in the next generation of her family, including assaults by male relatives on her own children. Writing her powerful book, *The Hidden Legacy*,[2] took years; her research required her to relive painful memories and explore her complicity, and she struggled with denial at every step of the way.

My daughter, Kate, came home from a vacation in Maine, the summer she was fifteen, with a broken heart. For the next several weeks, through the closed door of her room, I heard her pounding her typewriter. She emerged with a hundred-page memoir, titled "Beware Greeks Bearing Love." Eventually she allowed me to read it. It was a vivid, wickedly witty account of a summer love affair. I thought for a while that Kate might become a writer. She chose science instead and became a molecular biologist. (Both my children, growing up in a household supported precariously by writing, fled to the professions—my son, Tim, is an architect.) But at fifteen, halfway through high school, refining anger and disappointment into narrative, she wrote her first book.

I received so many letters from child-abuse survivors after I published *A Hole in the World*, and they told such extraordinary stories, that Ginger and I began discussing how we could incorporate them into a book. We decided to take a leaf from Studs Terkel and pursue a collective oral history. We wrote to some of the people who had written to me, won their agreement to be interviewed, and started taping interviews with them when we were traveling on other business. With the first interviews transcribed and edited, we prepared a book proposal and found a publisher. The book we're editing together will be Ginger's first, and its format—stories framed with comment—draws on her training as a radio journalist.

Ginger's a private pilot. Her flight instructor, Mike Goggins, a calm, trim young man, writes to fill the hours when he waits for clients on charter flights. He's writing something fictional. He hopes it might grow to be a novel. He read in a flying magazine about drug smugglers in Florida who recruit pilots to fly a load of drugs into the United States by offering to let them keep the plane. Mike wondered how a pilot's family would react if the pilot got caught. That question gave him his subject.

A publisher invited me to write my first book, *The Inland Ground,* even though I had never published a book or even a magazine article before. I broke into professional writing by writing book reviews. Conrad Knickerbocker, my mentor at Hallmark, had written reviews for the *Kansas City Star* and then moved on to reviewing for the old *New York Herald Tribune,* the *New York Times,* and *Life* magazine. When I told him I wanted to write, he recommended me to Thorpe Menn, the book review editor at the *Star.* Book review editors are always looking for reliable reviewers, so they're usually willing to take a chance on a newcomer. Menn gave me several books to try me out. He liked my work and began using me. (The *Star* paid for reviews in those days, the late 1960s, about what it had paid Ernest Hemingway for dispatches from France in 1918: fifteen dollars. I mentioned the coincidence to Menn. He pointed out that reviewers got to keep the book.)

After several years of reviewing for the *Star,* I accumulated enough reviews to send a selection of the best to *The New York Times Book Review* and the *Herald Tribune.* Both periodicals tried me out, liked my work, and added me to their list of active reviewers. They usually sent me fiction or verity connected in some way to life in the Midwest. To enliven my reviews I larded them with one-paragraph mini essays about the region, which is nearly as exotic a place to coastal natives as the Australian outback. To write is always to seal notes into bottles and cast them adrift at sea; you never know where your notes will drift and who will read them. I was editing a line of small gift books at Hallmark by then, getting paid to read Emerson and Thoreau and Ulysses S. Grant as well as poems about motherhood and the devotion of dogs. One day a man named Richard Kluger called me. He'd been editor of the *Herald Tribune* book section and was now a senior editor at Atheneum, the New York publishers. He'd noticed my reviews. I had a feeling for the Middle West, he said. He said there hadn't been a good book about the Midwest since *Winesburg, Ohio.* Would I consider submitting a proposal for such a book? Give me a couple of days to think about it, I responded.

Why wasn't Cinderella terrified when her fairy godmother appeared? I was terrified. I tried to convince myself that such a book was beyond me; the argument resulted in an outline instead. Atheneum accepted it, offered me a contract, and paid me a modest advance. I spent the advance, which sealed my commitment. I started researching and started trying to write, started therapy and started eating, and one weekend I went off on the coyote hunt that resulted in a story for *Esquire.* "Death All Day" became a chapter of *The Inland Ground,* which Atheneum published in 1970 and which was republished in a revised edition by the University Press of Kansas twenty years later.

These are only a few of the thousands of different ways people who want to write discover subjects, fictional or veritable, to write about. Subjects emerge from work, from hobbies and sports, from comments overheard at the next table, from public events, from travel, from private joys and sorrows, or simply from browsing the library. The best subject is always the subject that possesses you once you find it, that you can't stop thinking about.

It takes confidence to decide to write about a subject you haven't yet made your own. I knew very little about nuclear weapons when I decided to write a history of their development. I was doubtful that I'd ever master all the complex information I knew I'd find. I took the subject on, in 1979, because I was worried about the nuclear arms race and thought that going back to the beginning might help explain how our clever species had contrived to put itself in such mortal danger. I was forty-two in 1979, halfway through my life; I sensed that exploring the world's mortality might be a way of exploring my own.

"People seem not to see," writes Emerson, "that their opinion of the world is also a confession of character."

After four novels and two books of essays, I also felt ready to write a full-length historical narrative. Very few academic historians write such books anymore; their training, which has become analytic more than narrative, discourages them from doing so. From a practical point of view, I realized that there's a bigger market in the United States for verity than for fiction. My novels hadn't done that well; it was time for a change. Since that decision, my motto has been "Fools walk in where angels fear to tread." Certainly I felt foolish starting out.

"There's a recapitulation of the stages of the life cycle whenever you go to do something, [paint] a picture for example," the artist Joan Erikson, Erik Erikson's wife, told Mary Catherine Bateson. "You have to have a certain basic trust that you can do this—you are going to do this. You have to have will, you have to have imagination enough and fancy enough to do it your way, to make it unique. You have to have confidence, identity, and so on."[3] You need those virtues to write as well, but not all at once, *ab ovo.* Everyone feels like a tyro when she's starting something new. You gain confidence as you go along because you learn from your research and from actually solving the word-by-word, sentence-by-sentence problems of the work you've set for yourself.

Where you look for information depends on what you're planning to write about. When young people ask me how to get started writing, I tell them the best way would be to go somewhere and do something, experience something, and then write about it. That's how Hemingway got *The Sun Also Rises* and *A Farewell to Arms.* William Least Heat Moon took off on a grief trip after his wife walked out on him and kept notes and wrote *Blue Highways.* Herman Melville's first novels,

Typee and *Omoo,* drew on his experiences as an ordinary seaman on whaling ships, which led directly to his masterpiece, *Moby-Dick.* Henry David Thoreau stopped in the woods and built a cabin, not an obvious experience on which to base a book. ("If you advance confidently in the direction of your dreams," he wrote autobiographically in *Civil Disobedience,* "and endeavor to live the life you have imagined, you will meet with success unexpected in common hours.") You can easily add examples to this list. It helps to be young and unencumbered to go off and have experiences, but time and chance happen to us all. Aleksandr Solzhenitsyn turned ten terrible years of imprisonment and slave labor into *The Gulag Archipelago.* Michihiko Hachiya, a middle-aged physician at Hiroshima, kept a diary of his experiences treating the injured after the atomic bombing, published in English as *Hiroshima Diary.* I waited for the steadying perspective of middle age to write about my childhood in *A Hole in the World.* Sue Hubbell survived her forties in an Ozark cabin raising bees and transmuted the experience into her first book, *A Country Year.* Mary (M.F.K.) Fisher shaped her experiences with food and cooking into a form of memoir in the lifetime series of books collected together in *The Art of Eating.* Marguerite Duras waited until late middle age to write about the Chinese lover of her young adolescence in *The Lover*; in 1990, when she was seventy-six, she heard that he had died and wrote about him again in *The North China Lover.*

Document research is less exotic. The best way to learn document research is to take a college-level course in the subject. I never did, but I wish I had; my document research can be haphazard. There are always good books in print and in the library on how to do research. You might be able to coax a reference librarian into advising you or hire her services as an adviser part time. Reading other books about the subject you're exploring can be a good place to start. I'm an inveterate reader of footnotes, not only because they lead me to valuable further references and collections but also because academic historians often throw away priceless stories there. I ended Part One of *The Making of the Atomic Bomb* with a story about Enrico Fermi, the Italian physicist, standing at the window of his office high in the physics building at Columbia University, "looking down the gray winter length of Manhattan Island, its streets alive as always with vendors and taxis and crowds," thinking about the consequences of the discovery of nuclear fission: "He cupped his hands as if he were holding a ball. 'A little bomb like that,' he said simply . . . 'and it would all disappear.' "[4] I found this dramatic story, based on an eyewitness account, buried in a footnote in an academic history of the physics profession.

Starting research by reading other people's versions of the story you want to tell can give you a needed overview. It can also mislead you. If you read only *The Making of the Atomic Bomb*, you'd never realize that the Manhattan Project was riddled with Soviet spies, because I didn't credit the spy investigations of the immediate postwar years when I wrote that 1986 book. *Dark Sun* tells the espionage story. Since both my books are based on authentic sources, the second narrative doesn't invalidate the first, but it certainly enriches and complicates it.

Beginning research with original documents can sometimes be a better strategy. I plan, one of these days, to write about the Lewis and Clark expedition; I've already decided to begin my research for that work by reading the original expedition diaries rather than a historian's overview, to come fresh to the material and see the experience first through the explorers' eyes. Original documents are often the only information available on your subject; you may not have a choice of where to begin work.

Where are such documents to be found? They might be in your parents' attic or in the locked diaries your grandmother bequeathed you in her will, but they're probably on microfilm or microfiche or in the manuscript collections of a library somewhere. Look up bibliographies of your subject at the library; talk to reference librarians; check the books of other writers to see where they found their information. The U.S. Library of Congress has a vast collection of original documents; so does the National Archives; both are open to serious researchers with or without Ph.D.'s. (I have only a B.A., in history.) Local historical societies collect local history; they can be gold mines of documents on subjects not yet explored. Professional organizations collect materials relating to their profession; some, like the American Institute of Physics, also collect and transcribe oral histories. Courthouses and town halls are full of documents. So are old churches and museums.

Don't forget artifacts. Climbing around inside the Nagasaki B-29 was a valuable experience. So was being handed a spare leaf of gold foil from a set prepared to true the faces of the plutonium hemispheres of the Alamogordo bomb. If you're writing about skyscrapers or horses, you'd better go walk around one or sniff it and run your hand through its hair. One of the most powerful chapters in *The Inland Ground* is based on a two-hour tour of a Des Moines hog slaughterhouse. It's one thing to read Paul Gauguin's journals, another to stand in front of his great Tahitian-period paintings with their colors of volcanic earth and green tropical foliage, brown skin and dark blood. When I wrote a novel, *Sons of Earth,* about a returned astronaut whose son is kidnapped and held for ransom buried alive in a coffin fitted with a ventilation system, I designed and built the plywood coffin in my backyard; it spooked the hell out of my son.

I take notes on documents only when I can't make copies. That's not the way academic historians are taught to do research, but their style of writing is different from mine. I like to quote original sources extensively, letting the authentic voices of the participants tell the story; academic historians are trained to summarize. Since I don't know which passages I want to quote until I'm writing, I try whenever possible to take document copies home. That practice also saves time.

It's expensive to lodge in Washington, D.C., to work at the National Archives or the Library of Congress. When U.S. astronauts explored the moon, their first assignment upon leaving the moon lander was to grab what NASA called a "contingency sample" of moon rocks, in case their equipment malfunctioned and they had to blast off. Out-of-town document research is contingent as far as I'm concerned; I skim files and make copies of everything that looks even remotely useful (or mark it to have it copied) rather than read each document carefully through. I can read everything carefully when I'm back home. For the same reason—to have them at hand when I'm writing—I buy out-of-print books important to my research in second-hand bookstores. Many such books can be ordered by phone at reasonable prices from the Strand Bookstore in New York. Sometimes copying documents isn't allowed. If notes won't do, you can type the document contents into a portable computer or dictate them into a tape recorder. But make copies of documents if you can; often their physical form reveals information beyond what's in their contents—a Founding Father's handwriting, the original security clearance, stains, significant corrections.

Sooner or later, unless your subject is distantly historical, you'll have to go interviewing. The problem for amateurs (and sometimes for independent professionals as well) is getting your foot in the door. Secretaries are gatekeepers; treat them with the respect they deserve. Most people will give you an interview if they perceive you to be serious. The best way to encourage that perception is to be prepared, to seem to know what you are talking about. The best way to prepare yourself is to do your homework in books and documents first. People like to talk about their work; most people want to be acknowledged and remembered. Tell them what you're doing and why you need to talk to them. To the extent that you can do so accurately and comfortably, discuss the subject of their expertise in the jargon of their occupation. I've finally reached a point where I can talk a little physics; it helps. Many experts are also teachers, predisposed to explain. Elected officials got where they are by selling themselves to voters; if they don't try to sell themselves to you, call in the paramedics. Dress appropriately. Arrive on time. Go about the interview in a businesslike way. Don't use more time than your interviewee allotted, unless he obviously wants to continue.

Different interview situations require different tools. Some people don't bat an eye at a tape recorder; others clam up. Always ask permission to tape. I usually explain, "It's a good way to take notes." If I'm pressed I emphasize tape's superior accuracy. Tape size doesn't matter except that microcassettes are easier to lug around airports. Ginger uses standard cassettes (they're sturdier) and a special paddle-shaped microphone that picks up sound from the surface it's resting on. It's unobtrusive; people forget it's there. It's sensitive to voices but insensitive to ambient noise. The omnidirectional condenser mike built into most tape recorders is a last resort at best. *Always install fresh batteries before an interview.* Taping substitutes for memory. You rely on the machine to remember for you while you're thinking ahead to the next question you want to ask. If the batteries in your recorder fail, you've lost an interview that may contain statements crucial to your research and that you've invested scarce time and money to collect. Batteries are cheaper. Save the used ones for clocks and flashlights if you're frugal.

When I was preparing to work with a Missouri farmer to research my book *Farm,* I called Tracy Kidder for advice. Tracy follows people for months before he writes about them. I asked him how he took notes. "Don't try to tape-record," he told me. "People freeze up, and besides, it'd take years to transcribe all that tape. I just buy a stack of pocket-size spiral notebooks and make notes whenever I can." I stopped at the corner drugstore on my way through Higginsville, Missouri, to the farm where I'd be working and bought a stack of little notebooks and a handful of ballpoint pens. The farmers I got to know took my notebooks so much for granted that I was able eventually to write down their dialogue verbatim while they talked. Once, at an auction, I was leaning against a combine, making notes on all the people looking over the farm machines. A farmer noticed me scribbling away furiously and came over and waited for me to look up. "Did you get that last bid?" he asked.

Truman Capote claimed to have trained himself to remember up to four hours' interviewing word for word, a skill he cultivated so that he could interview the imprisoned murderers of *In Cold Blood* without spooking them. I believe him. More than once I've run to my rental car and disgorged whole conversations onto tape. David Halberstam, who often pursues people who don't want to talk and won't talk where a record is being kept, does interviews that way.

It helps if you know your subject. Then statements made in interviews fit into slots in a familiar framework. That's the way waiters remember twelve orders around a table without writing them down: by attaching you and your order mentally to objects in a familiar landscape. Harry Gold, an American chemist who served as a courier for Soviet atomic espionage during the Second World War, recalled his hundreds of rendezvous so minutely that skeptics accused him of making them up. The truth is, he was a sports fanatic; he remembered espionage dates so well because he keyed them to sporting events.

It's much less expensive to interview people over the phone than to travel to talk to them personally, but you lose the information of your other senses when you do. If you want only information, not an impression of someone's presence, then the phone works reasonably well. Be sure you get permission *on tape* if you want to tape the conversation. In some states it's illegal to tape-record a phone conversation without the other party's knowledge; if she agrees on tape, you have evidence that you complied with the law.

Transcribing tape is hard work. If you can hire it out, by all means do so. Some tapes are too poor in quality, too private, or too dense with jargon, to turn over to a transcribing service. Those you'll have to do yourself. Don't erase or record over your tapes; you may need them as evidence in a libel suit.

Whenever possible, I organize document series in notebooks. They're easier to study that way. Merging documents from different sources chronologically can reveal sequences and patterns that you might miss if you worked with them separately.

It can help to organize a chronological notebook. If you're writing history, your reader will expect a clear chronology, however you structure your narrative. The chronology for *Dark Sun* extends to more than a thousand pages. I worked with it simultaneously on-screen and in notebook form. Under each date, I blocked in either the actual primary source material from which I expected to quote or a reference to a book or file document. The chronology became the skeleton of my book. Reference your chronology carefully if you plan to footnote your work. It was maddening to find apt quotations adrift in my chronology with missing attributions; once or twice I wasted hours tracking down an obscure attribution I'd forgotten to list.

I had so much reference material when I prepared to write *The Making of the Atomic Bomb*—several hundred books and three file drawers crammed with documents—that I needed some system for indexing it all. In those analog days I turned to the tidy system graduate students used of ruled six-by-nine cards punched around the perimeter with rows of numbered holes. I indexed the information I typed onto the cards by a number system that related topics to holes. The cards came with a notching punch. If an index subject appeared on a card, I notched open the appropriate hole. I ended up with about twelve hundred cards. According to theory, you could line up the cards, slide a knitting needle through a hole, shake the stack, and shake out the cards notched for that topic. The system worked as advertised if you had only forty or fifty cards, but my stack was thick as a paving stone. It took me an hour or more to shake loose cards on a single topic. That was still better than sorting through documents by hand.

With *Dark Sun* I decided to try to find a computerized database system that would do what my cards had done but do it quickly and electronically. I dreamed of scanning documents electronically into my computer, loading them into a database system, and retrieving references instantly at the click of a mouse. But optical character recognition systems are still so inaccurate that it takes more time to correct their mistakes than it would to type in the data you're trying to scan. And most database systems limit the length of document, so they can't handle complete texts. The one system I found that accepts documents of any length is called, eccentrically, "ask Sam." Many people use it. I wish I could say it worked for me. It meant well, but when I tried to copy quotations over from "ask Sam" to my word-processing program, it usually crashed the program. I entered some of my documents into "ask Sam," and I use it, cautiously, after I'm sure I've backed up my text. The best document-indexing system I've found is the chronology I organized. When I want to look something up, I use my word processor's Search function.

Good writing is all handmade. It's made of words. Looking up words as you write is a vital step in research. A word choice isn't apt merely because a word's formal definition seems to fit. Words are layered with meaning, and the layers need to fit as well. If you write "the final solution to our problem" unaware that "final solution" translates the Nazi euphemism for the Holocaust, *die Endlösung;* if you write "a supercilious handshake" unaware that "supercilious" derives from Latin words meaning "above the eyelid" (i.e., with a lifted eyebrow), you communicate more and less to your reader than you intend. Sloppy word choice isn't only a literary sin; it's confusing. If you choose words with their multileveled meanings in mind, your reader will have a better chance of understanding what you mean—and so will you.

E. Annie Proulx, who won the 1994 Pulitzer Prize for Fiction for her novel *The Shipping News,* studied the *Dictionary of Newfoundland English* to learn the dialect she wanted her characters to speak. "I literally slept with that book for two years, in the bed," she told an interviewer. "I'd fall asleep while I was reading it. This is the point in work. You get it right, or you don't do it. Everything depends on your getting it right."[5]

Words derive ultimately from the body, the ground and only vessel of experience. The body extends itself into the world by imitation and analogy. The hand grasping an object, the ear and eye and nose and tongue grasping an object, make a negative of the object, an imitation, a mold. The molds are stored in memory and accumulate. Eventually they assemble an image even in the object's absence. The image replaces the object and constructs continuity. Thus the body modifies the world and captures it, making it available for thought, for language, and for alteration.

The oldest words we know, the old Indo-European roots, were concrete and bodily: *djku,* sweet; *dub,* to drop; *drem,* to sleep; *el,* red; *esen,* harvest; *er,* earth; *ere,* to row. Analogy—metaphor—elaborated them, one end anchored still in the body, the other end a fishing rod cast out into the world. Indo-European *ker*—heat, fire—whence carbon and cremate and ceramic. Indo-European *kelp*—to hold, to grasp—whence helm and halberd and halter. *Ghei*—to yawn—whence yawn and chasm and grasp and gill. *Angh*—tight, painfully constricted—whence nail, anger, anguish, angina. *Sta*[*h*]—to stand, that which stands—whence this bounty: steed and stud, stool, stow, stage, stanza, statue, arrest, circumstance, contrast, cost, distant, oust, obstacle, substitute, superstition, standard, armistice, starling and state, sta-

tistics and starboard and steer, store and restore, assist and consist and exist and persist, apostasy and epistemology and prostate and stoic and post.

The most accurate information about a word's history is a compilation of how it's been used since it first appeared in print. Dictionaries organized historically provide such compilations. The preeminent historical source for English is the *Oxford English Dictionary.* A less cumbersome source (unless you have the *OED* on CD-ROM) is the *American Heritage Dictionary,* which at least gives condensed etymologies. I frequently look up ten or fifteen different, related words before I find one that clicks into place and locks down my meaning.

People who don't like to use dictionaries argue that readers don't know the histories of words. Some readers do and find it difficult to read what you write if you choose words carelessly (and there aren't so many devoted readers left in the world that you can afford to alienate them). But even if most readers didn't know, *the language knows.* It's not a collection of distinct objects; it's an interconnected network, a structure like a geodesic dome, where every part supports* every other. For evidence, to end this long chapter, I offer a paragraph from my memoir, *A Hole in the World.* It links a childhood experience most of us have forgotten with the progress of a thunderstorm, the storm words serving to reactivate in the reader the felt experience of learning to read that time has quieted:

> Once I learned to read I was launched, adrift in dreamtime half the rest of my life. I had already seen past appearances, ants boiling up from the joints in concrete sidewalks, trees tied in knots, limestone compacted of the lives of uncountable billions of individual shells, the burst of saliva in my mouth when Betsy

* *sub* + *portare,* "to carry from below." My first draft had "depends upon," but that gave *de* + *pend,* "to hang down." Geodesic domes don't work by hanging down; they work by supporting.

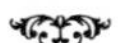

poured vinegar to rinse Lois's hair, the space my mother should have occupied rent like a tear in the fabric of time. Now I saw—because Mrs. Gernhardt started me and my vernacular brother guided me to fluency—that words could boil up worlds that towered overhead like a spring storm, splashed light and shadow the length and width of a city, drove crowds under cover, crashed lightning, uprooted trees, flooded streets, stopped traffic, rumbled away in a passage of cold wind and abruptly dissipated, pure energy, nothing left but clean air and the bright sun shining. That real, that profligate, that leviathan, and all of it open to me without restraint in the pages of books, pouring out into my child's life like Niagara.[6]

Five

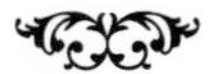

THE SHAPE OF THINGS TO COME: I

Having done the necessary research, having explored a possible voice through which to tell the story, how do you shape the work? How do you get from notes and a voice to a short story or an article, to a novel or a book?

I doubt if many professional writers prepare a formal outline, except perhaps as part of a book proposal in pursuit of an advance payment to fund the work of writing. I know I don't. I make notes as I go along, usually a notepad list of the points I want to touch on or the events I want to include within a story or within a chapter of a book. But organizing information isn't the same as structuring a work of writing. Structuring a work of writing is more like generalship. A general needs to know what troops and weapons he commands and how they're deployed, but he also needs to develop a strategy for fighting battles and winning the war. The battles probably won't go as he plans, of course. If his strategy is sufficiently flexible, he'll be able to adapt it to circumstances and still come out victorious.

To change the metaphor: strategy—figuring out a structure—is a craft skill that you use to fashion your raw materials into a shaped, finished work. The raw materials of writing are never completely plastic; they always resist shaping and force you to adapt your plan to their limitations. Writing historical fiction felt to me like working wood. The recorded facts of the Donner story, which I had decided not to deviate from, gave grain and direction to the writing, limiting the extent to which I could shape the characters and the story. Writing fiction improvisationally, as novelists more typically do and as I did with my novels *Holy Secrets, The Last Safari,* and *Sons of Earth,* felt like working clay: plastic at first, since I was making up the story rather than basing it on real events, but increasingly resistant as the clay dried out. As the story progressed, that is, the characters became increasingly defined and the requirement that they be consistent with the "facts" of their existence limited their range of action. Writing history, on the other hand, is similar to accounting: you enter facts into the accounting system you've devised and support each entry with a document delivered into the system from the real world. I was going to say writing history is more creative than that, but then we've all heard about how creative accounting can be.

There's no formal school, so far as I know, where you can learn how to structure long forms of prose. Writing programs typically work with short forms, for the obvious reason that short forms can be examined productively within the brief compass of a course program. But the difference between long forms and short forms is precisely their structure, which means that you can't learn how to structure the one by studying the other. Fortunately, you can teach yourself long-form structure by reading books and analyzing how their authors assembled them.

Again and again, with short forms and with long, you'll find that writers structure their work not on the basis of some abstract, predetermined scheme but practically, to solve problems their materials present. (Henry James's justly celebrated prefaces to his collected works, published together as *The Art of the Novel,* demonstrate that practical approach to writing.) *Tristram Shandy,* for example, is a satire of intellectual rigidity. If Sterne set out to write such a satire, he probably found his reversible-book joke when he tried to decide whether to begin *ab ovo* or *in medias res* and realized that those traditional schemas were also intellectually rigid: why not give the reader a choice? By doing so, he was able to extend his satire to the formal structure of the book itself, adding another layer of performance to the work. The more you can make the different elements of writing work together, the more effective your writing will be. If the elements of a work (character, voice, story, structure, and so on) reinforce each other—play out chordally rather than simply contrapuntally—then you get resonant overtones that engage readers more profoundly by enlarging the work's range of intellectual and emotional reference. It's difficult to plan such resonances ahead of time as an abstract exercise. You find them as you solve the practical problems of writing.

You do have to decide early on in a particular project, if not at the outset, what traditional form you want to use. (You probably decided that even before you began research, but writers sometimes aren't sure.) Given the ideas and information you have at hand, are you going to write an essay, a short story, a magazine article, a book-length work of verity, a novel, or something else? Each has its own formal requirements, which make switching from one to the other along the way difficult. (That limitation applies on the large scale of writing careers as well as on the smaller scale of individual works. Many writers who train in writing programs hone their skills on short stories, expecting to switch over later to writing novels. Some make the transition; many don't. The forms aren't the same. Such writers might have been better off learning to write long fiction from the beginning, as self-taught novelists usually do. Newspaper journalists frequently have the same difficulty—trouble with the form—transitioning to writing books. Screenwriters who write coherent scenes frequently can't sustain the coherence across the one hundred twenty pages of a screenplay; how many movies have you seen that fall apart in the second half?)

Forms require different orchestrations that prevent them from being interchangeable. We read that a work of verity has been "novelized" to protect the writer from a libel suit, but the resulting book works only for those who are in on the secret—who know that President Studley is "really" John Kennedy and Kelly Brasize is "really" Marilyn Monroe. Screenplays are often "novelized" as well, but as novels they're sketchy; they work for those who saw the movie and can supply its visual and aural orchestration from memory. It's such a truism that good novels don't make good movies that you can almost judge the "novelism" of a novel by that rule. Despite the dreams of youth, song lyrics don't make good poems. A song lyric depends on the music for its orchestration and looks skinny and naked alone on the page unless you hum the tune. A poem, which must enter the world unaccompanied, arrives fat with verbal orchestration. A poem gets its comeuppance in turn when it's stuck on a greeting card, where it looks overweight and overdressed. Greeting card verse, at which true poets jeer, works in a greeting card because the card's design and illustration supply its necessary orchestration, much as music does for a song lyric.

The best single book on the formal structures of writing is Northrop Frye's masterful analysis, *Anatomy of Criticism,* which every writer should read. I have a copy I bought in January 1959, my senior year in college; I've returned to it regularly for guidance for more than three decades. Frye clarifies the relationship between short and long forms of fiction and verity, for example, with this helpful proportion:

short story: novel = essay: autobiography.

The short story, that is, isn't just a scene from a novel but a different form entirely that's related to the novel, just as the essay isn't just a chapter from an autobiography but is nevertheless related to autobiography. I've written all four forms, and I can confirm Frye's observation from experience: each form sets its own limitations and makes its own demands. When I quoted Gabriel García Márquez on the difficulty of beginning a novel, I left out part of the quotation, which concerned short-story writing. "The effort involved in writing a short story is as intense as beginning a novel," García Márquez also wrote. ". . . But a [short] story has no beginning, no end: either it works or it doesn't." That distinction defines the difference between a short story and a scene from a novel from the point of view of a writer at work. In García Márquez's experience, writing a short story is something like writing the beginning of a novel—dense, allusive, pyrotechnic. Which helps explain why the short story is such a resonant form: all that follows in a novel, all the elaboration of story and character—the long middle and the brief, resolving end—is held latent in a good short story, left for the reader to fill in from imagination and from personal experience. It's not surprising that good short stories haunt us.

I've been interested for some years in the long prose form that includes such works as *Gulliver's Travels, Candide, Tristram Shandy, Moby-Dick, Alice in Wonderland,* James Joyce's *Ulysses,* Aldous Huxley's *Brave New World,* and George Orwell's *1984*. Works of this type are usually shoved in under the rubric "novel," Frye points out, since they're evidently fictional, but are then criticized for all the extra baggage they carry—diversions of various kinds, "two-dimensional" characters, fanciful and unrealistic events, abrupt stylistic changes, and, often, extensive inclusions of real or imitation "factual" material, such as the pages of quotations at the beginning of *Moby-Dick*. I once looked up contemporary reviews of *Moby-Dick,* published in 1851, and of *Ulysses,* published in 1922, and found two reviewers seventy-one years apart who used the same word to condemn each book. The word applied to these monumental works of literature was "midden"—a dunghill, a pile of trash. Even some modern critics complain that *Moby-Dick* would benefit from trimming; they want to make it more like a novel.

Frye had the good sense to see that works of the kind I've listed have more in common with each other than with the novel; he identifies them as a long prose form different from the novel. I won't draw a point-by-point comparison—you can read that in Frye—but will say only that he offers Oxford clergyman Robert Burton's 1621 prose work *The Anatomy of Melancholy* as the type specimen of the form and proposes that such books be called anatomies. He obviously intended to identify his own *Anatomy of Criticism* as an example of the form, which can shape a work of verity as well as of fiction. "At its most concentrated," Frye writes, "the [anatomy] presents us with a vision of the world in terms of a single intellectual pattern. The intellectual structure built up from the story makes for violent dislocations in the customary logic of narrative, though the appearance of carelessness that results reflects only the carelessness of the reader or his tendency to judge by a novel-centered conception of fiction."[1]

Deciding which form to use isn't only a practical or personal decision; it's also a strategic decision. The long forms aren't direct extensions of the short. An elusive moment that might make a powerful short story can't be simply enlarged into a novel. Think about your favorite short story and try to imagine it at novel length. An idea that works at essay length—my two-hour tour of a Des Moines slaughterhouse, for example—would founder at book length. Similarly, a book furnished with a story that's too small feels padded (though size is always relative to the number of connections the writer is able to make; it's possible, in William Blake's words, "to see a world in a grain of sand").

I first encountered the Donner Party story as one of several parallel narratives woven together in Bernard DeVoto's book *The Year of Decision: 1846*. I explored it further in George R. Stewart's history *Ordeal by Hunger*. Both books told me in great detail what had happened to the Donner families, but neither book resolved my questions about how the men and women and children came to their suffering and how it changed them. Since I wanted to understand an aspect of the story that was factually unrecoverable from the historical record, I looked next for novels based on the Donner experience. As I recall, I found two, but one was insufferably glib, eliminating the cannibalism entirely and turning the story into a clichéd western, and the other bizarrely offered as its central character and hero Lewis Keseberg, a dark, monstrous German who was accused by his contemporaries of killing Tamsen Donner, the matriarch of the Donner clan, for fresh meat. As usual, the book I was looking for hadn't been written yet. Sometimes I think writers are people who run out of good books to read and decide in desperation to write their own. (If that's your game, beware: writing makes you a more discriminating reader, which correspondingly reduces the number of books you can bear to read.)

Structurally, the problem with the Donner Party experience was that it didn't begin until halfway through the story. The eighty-three people who became the Donner Party were simply emigrants moving west from farms and small towns in the East and on the Middle Border until they were forced to take refuge high in the mountains when early snow closed the Sierra passes. Yet the events prior to the time they fell into that collective hole were important to understanding why the Donners failed when so many others, that year and in later years, made the crossing into California successfully. Arrogant decisions and bad luck propelled the Donner Party to its fate, which is why the story felt like a collective Greek tragedy. I wanted those moments of tragic peripeteia on the record, but I also wanted to get to the mountains and begin the real story as quickly as possible.

The diary form argued for beginning at the beginning. I could certainly have looped even that form around to begin the story in the mountains, perhaps on November 3, when the Donner Party woke to find the passes closed, and could then have cut back to the beginning and hauled the group across the prairie from Independence to November. Other considerations convinced me not to loop the chronology but to start the diary *ab ovo.*

First, there were simply too many characters to introduce. The slow passage across the prairie gave me time to introduce them in action as they joined the larger wagon train and then the Donner Party, family by family, like tributary streams coming together to make a river. Second, modern readers would have difficulty appreciating the full horror of the snow-blocked passes without preparation—they needed to know what came before so that they would know there was no place to retreat. Finally, I wanted to write a work of fiction with historical verisimilitude, and cutting what I meant to sound like an old diary back and forth in a modern, cinematic way would disrupt that illusion. I'd chosen Clyman's voice to tell the story for the same reason, to make the narrative itself feel authentically old.

So the structure I settled on for *The Ungodly* was a diary, written in an "authentic" voice that was nevertheless omniscient, that began *ab ovo* back in Illinois on March 26, 1846, when George Donner first placed an advertisement for teamsters in the *Sangamo Journal.* And because I understood that the first part of the story, however necessary, was so much clutter on the porch of the central plot, I confined Part One, which I called "The Trail," to a series of brief entries, with a few long entries to report important events. Though the journey across the prairie and the desert was chronologically more than half the story, I covered it in the first 81 pages of a 370-page novel. If the Donners were in a race for the Sierra passes, so was I.

My editor saw the structural problem immediately, by the way, and we talked it out at length. He concurred in my arrangement, but I have no doubt that the decision to structure the story as I did cost me readers. It blew right by the *New York Times Book Review* reviewer, a fictioneer named Michael Malone who now writes soap operas, who complained that you don't write novels by following a story *exactly.* I thought that was a fatuous criticism then and still do. You write novels any way you want—any way you can make them work.

Having worked within a rigid structure with *The Ungodly,* I deliberately set out with my second novel, *Holy Secrets,* to learn to write fiction improvisationally. I had a one-sentence version of the story I meant to tell: A surgeon, married to a passionate but violent and alcoholic woman, discovers that she has been unfaithful to him, divorces her, goes through a period of grieving, meets another woman, and falls in love again. Within that broad compass I sat down to let the story tell itself. It was a great pleasure to improvise after turning the relentless twelve-page-a-day mill wheel of the Donner story. I had an advance from a publisher sufficient to buy a less constricted space of time.

The surgeon's story took the shape of a descent to a low point—the breakdown of his marriage and the divorce—followed by an ascent back up to normal life again. As soon as I graphed the plot that way mentally, I saw Dante's physical progress through the Inferno: from the surface of the earth down to the bottom of Hell and then back up to earth again. It was this realization of the structure of the story that gave me the novel's first line, "Lost in the middle of life," which alludes to the first line of the *Inferno* ("In the middle of the journey to our life I came to myself within a dark wood where the straight way was lost"). After that, as I improvised the narrative, I kept this simple but evocative structure in mind. I alluded to Dante only once more in the entire book. The breakdown of a marriage may feel to the people involved like a descent into hell, so I didn't mind borrowing the Dantean aura, but equating my surgeon's modest domestic tragedy more explicitly with Christianity's great human tragedy would have been grandiose.

The concatenate curve of its plot, like a chain suspended from two points, gave *Holy Secrets* an odd shape. Usually a story builds to a peak,

a climax, and then descends to an ending. The inverted shape of my plot dictated a corresponding emotional structure to the story: violence, anger, rage descending to depression and introspection, followed by a slow ascent to love (it helped, of course, that this shape had its counterpart in ordinary experience—many readers would recognize it, and I had just descended through divorce and was ascending in love myself). Clearly this was a story to tell entirely from the surgeon's point of view, but because of the problem I had with hearing the first person singular as my own voice, I chose indirect first person instead.

Once my journalistic persona stopped nagging me that sitting still free-associating was wasting time, improvising was a pleasure. In those days I made my living writing magazine articles, selling as many as seven a year to such national magazines as *Harper's*, *Esquire*, *Playboy*, and the *Atlantic*. Working up a magazine article every month kept me jumping. I collected information, organized it mentally, sat down, and forced the words to form. Any logjams I encountered I pried at in the dark before sleep; usually I woke in the morning to find the timber flowing with the river again. *Holy Secrets* was different. Populating my novel with invented characters, visualizing scenes at my typewriter with my eyes closed and transferring them to the page, working an hour or more on a single sentence to get the words right, were luxuries I had not previously been able to afford.

I don't know how other writers invent scenes. I use controlled meditation. Meditation to me means not the mind-emptying repetition of a nonsense mantra but focused visualization, the kind of meditation that used to be recommended to the Christian devout. In John Donne's time there were tracts on meditation; he followed their precepts in composing his *Holy Sonnets*. Christian meditation began with a Bible verse on which the meditator was supposed to focus his attention. After he had the verse well in mind, he then closed his eyes and visualized a setting for it. "The Lord is my shepherd" produced a pasture, sheep, a benevolent shepherd. This part was called "composition of place." (In Donne's poems it often occurs in the first line: "Batter my heart, three-person'd God"; "At the round earth's imagined corners"). Manipulations then followed as the meditator brought the scene to life and inserted himself into it. In effect, the process animated a Bible verse into a virtual reality, so that its meaning acted itself out dramatically in the mental space of the devout.

I use the same process to visualize fictional scenes and to reconstruct historical events, installing the scene or event in a mental space where I can manipulate it imaginatively. Doing so takes concentration, but it rewards that effort by giving you an immediate check on the plausibility of your inventions or suppositions. Sometimes the scenes almost seem to play themselves as the preconscious part of the mind feeds in improvisations. Then it's hard to type fast enough to get it all down (which is a rewarding reason for learning to touch-type). What you write down is usually no more than a rough sketch; you still have a long course of work refining your choice of words.

Eventually, *Holy Secrets* found its way to the actor Donald Sutherland, who saw a possible lead role in its surgeon. After Sutherland had read the novel we talked on the phone. "It has two female leads," the actor told me almost immediately. "Can't have two female leads. You'll have to choose one or the other. Call me when you decide which one, and we'll talk some more." I realized he was right, but I also realized that dropping the wife or the new lover would make a different story, with a different shape. I didn't want to crank my emotions around to write another story based on a story I'd already written. I never placed that call.

In 1973, I traveled to East Africa on assignment to write about the place where our species first evolved. I'd traveled in the United States with Richard Leakey, the Kenyan paleontologist, when he was here lecturing, and called on him at the National Museum in Nairobi. Then I hired a Land-Rover and a Kikuyu driver and spent two weeks following the game circuit through Serengeti National Park, visiting Olduvai Gorge, where Leakey's parents had worked, and the Eden of animals that graze in the broad caldera of Ngorongoro Crater. East Africa is the last place on earth where it's possible to see what the world was like before human cultivation. The Serengeti reminded me of the western prairie, with wildebeest by the millions instead of buffalo.

After I returned home, I began reading about East Africa. Hemingway's *Green Hills of Africa,* a nonfiction novel published decades before anyone coined that term, particularly impressed me. I'd found Hemingway hard to read when I was younger. Now, because I'd done some writing myself, I realized what an exceptional craftsman he was. I reread his major novels to try to understand how he put them together. (I noticed one day, looking over *For Whom the Bell Tolls,* that Hemingway's care with his work extended even to the beginnings of chapters: no two chapters in the novel began with sentences of the same structure, a fine touch of finish. He must have gone through at the end and carefully checked each one.)

Because so many younger sons of English nobility had shipped for East Africa in its early days to pioneer, there was a rich East African literature in English. The indigenous cultures were ancient and complex as well—the Kikuyu, the exotic Masai. Our species evolved in the Rift Valley. I decided to set a novel in East Africa. I wanted to tell the story of a good man who gives up his life to save the life of the woman he loves. At the time that seemed like an original idea. I see now that I borrowed it from *For Whom the Bell Tolls.* I would write the novel, *The Last Safari,* in homage to Hemingway, deliberately evoking Hemingway's style. The good man would be an American white hunter of missionary parents, Seth Crown, who operated a tent camp in Serengeti National Park. A subplot would involve a young American paleontologist working at a site nearby like Olduvai Gorge. Guerrillas would attack the tent camp. Eventually they would kidnap Crown's girlfriend and offer to exchange her for him. He would walk to the guerrilla camp and discover that their leader, Rukuma, was his estranged half-African son. Crown's son would kill him; the police would raid the camp and rescue the woman Crown saved; the son would escape. The paleontologist would find an important new hominid skull and name the species *Homo regulus,* "man crowned." Hemingway himself would make a brief appearance in a story within a story that Crown would tell, passing a charging rhino bullfighter-style with a camp-blanket cape.

I set to work trying to find a voice that could tell this tale. I tried eight or ten opening chapters from Crown's point of view. I tried four or five from the paleontologist's point of view and another two or three from the girlfriend's. Nothing worked. I had more than six weeks to write this novel, but I didn't have forever. I'd bought a summer with the signing advance, thinking I'd be able to move the novel well along, but summer was getting well along instead, and all I had to show were some twenty unworkable drafts of chapter one. Every time another approach failed, my depression darkened. My old flirtation with suicide returned—not because I was depressed, it seems to me now, but as a release from the total frustration I felt.

And then one day I saw what was wrong. Any high-school writing teacher would have realized immediately what the problem was. I'd written four and published two novels, each narrated in a single voice. A single voice couldn't tell *The Last Safari.* The separate parts were too far apart, culturally as well as geographically: Crown, his girlfriend, the paleontologist, the various Africans, most of all his opponent, Rukuma, and Rukuma's guerrilla band. Eureka. I needed *multiple* voices. It was truly stupid, I told myself, not to have seen that my

problem was structural. I sat down and started writing. I used indirect first person, but shifted the voice from character to character as the narrative moved along:

> Two Masai herdboys found the head. It was rolled away from the body as if someone had kicked it and it had been severed cleanly with a panga or a sword. . . .
>
> Crown was driving too fast. He knew most of the people in the district, African as well as European, and it enraged him that one of them might be dead. . . .
>
> Ole Senkali was the father of the two herdboys. When his son came running into the *manyatta* he had been playing the board game of stones and holes with his father-in-law. . . .
>
> The girl's name was Cassie Wendover. She had come out to East Africa from California and found Crown at his tent camp south of Serengeti National Park and taken up with him and she still wondered at her luck. . . .[2]

And so on, one character handing off the story to the next, with the Hemingwayesque voice in indirect first person smoothing the seams. Small changes in diction and vocabulary served to identify each speaker. I had a good first chapter in a matter of days. The system of multiple voices telling the story, like a Studs Terkel oral history, shaped a structure as it went along, allowing the story to shift from place to place and event to event naturally as the eyewitnesses reported what they experienced and what they thought. I killed Crown off twenty-seven pages from the end of the book; Cassie told most of the rest of the story. If Crown had narrated the novel he'd have had to survive, like Ishmael.

If I overdid the Hemingway, it was certainly fun to do and a learning experience as well. Fools walk in. Writing a book is always a gamble; why not increase the stakes? I stopped writing realistic novels after I'd published four because I'd fallen into a routine and had begun repeating myself. When I return to fiction, a return I've been planning for more than ten years, I'll try something completely different from what I did before. At the moment, I'm still learning how to write long works of verity.

Six

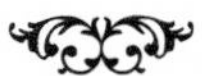

THE SHAPE OF THINGS TO COME: II

For structural reasons, Seth Crown in *The Last Safari* needed a sidekick, a friend who could share the story when Crown's lover, Cassie Wendover, was elsewhere, someone who connected Crown's past to his present. I invented a Somali named Abdi, who had worked with Crown in their hunting-safari days and who now managed Crown's Serengeti tent camp. Abdi emerged into the narrative one day complete and entire, asking Crown to pick up a load of pink Chinese toilet paper in Arusha for the tent camp after he dropped off the body of the murdered man with the Arusha police. From the beginning, I knew Abdi well—who he was, where he came from, how he spoke, what his values were. Crown quotes him to Cassie, telling the story of Boer settlers raping and murdering Rukuma's mother, Crown's first wife. I read that narrative to an audience at a writers' conference. No one breathed from beginning to end, which told me I had the character right.

Where do characters come from? How do you invent them? Shortly after the maverick psychologist Julian Jaynes published his curious book, *The Origin of Consciousness in the Breakdown of the Bicameral Mind*, in 1976, I arranged to interview him in Princeton, where he taught, for a magazine profile. I can't speak to the validity of Jaynes's theories about consciousness, but one point he made in the interview helped me understand where characters come from. "Psychology will never be a science," Jaynes told me, "until it can explain *acting*." How does an actor "become" another character? For some it's a highly conscious process, for others more emotional and osmotic, yet once they've worked up a role, they learn to switch over almost effortlessly into a mental state where they respond differently from how they normally respond. The haunting is voluntary. They're still themselves. Anthony Hopkins, interviewed about playing the cannibal psychiatrist Hannibal Lecter in the movie *The Silence of the Lambs,* hinted mockingly but I think also seriously that he summoned the fictional persona from murky and dangerous personal depths. If he consumed fava beans and a fine Chianti to prepare for the part, he didn't, to my knowledge, consume anyone's liver.

Inventing fictional characters, I understood after interviewing Julian Jaynes, was like improvisational acting. All your characters are you, virtuals of you; writing is a controlled process of splitting into virtual personalities in the safe haven of the page. I can't tell you how to do that except to say that it feels like self-hypnosis and probably is. Controlled meditation helps. Once you've invented a character and gotten to know her, you relax into the role and she appears. In a long interview published in book form in 1994, the screenwriter and director Ingmar Bergman describes how he created the personae for his 1969 film *The Ritual* out of the conflicted parts of his own identity:

> I divided myself into three characters. . . . Sebastian Fischer is irresponsible, lecherous, unpredictable, infantile . . . epicurean, lazy, amiable, soft and brutal. Hans Winkelmann, on the other hand, is orderly, strictly disciplined with a deep sense of responsibility, socially aware, good-humored and patient. The woman, Thea . . . is unbearably sensitive—cannot even stand to wear clothes at times.[1]

Some characters are easier to do than others. Some never come alive (presumably because they don't resonate for you); you have to move them around like robots or, better, replace them. If you have trouble with a character, try F. Scott Fitzgerald's approach: write a profile of the character for your own use or make lists of his likes and dislikes, of his opinions and tastes. Watch out for characters like Abdi, who appear fully formed; they're the ones writers mean when they say a character threatens to take over their story. They're the ones on television and in movies who spawn spin-offs. Years after I wrote *The Last Safari,* I realized where Abdi came from. I grew up before the coming of television. We listened to radio serials instead—*Jack Armstrong, The Shadow.* One that I cherished was *The Lone Ranger.* The Lone Ranger's sidekick was a loyal, wise, honest, sometimes wry Native American named Tonto. Abdi was Tonto, a voice out of my childhood.

Like everything else in writing, characters are made of words. You distinguish them one from another first of all by how they speak. I received a Guggenheim Fellowship in 1974 to write a novel set at the secret atomic bomb laboratory at Los Alamos, New Mexico, during the Second World War. I decided to cast the entire novel as a dialogue between a troubled physicist and his psychoanalyst (I won't bore you explaining why I chose such an awkward structure for my novel; it seemed like a good idea at the time). When I read a chapter of my work in progress at a writers' conference, I found I had to insert "said X" and "said Y" repeatedly to distinguish between the two characters' voices in dialogue. After the reading, a poet who teaches writing professionally took me aside. "The characters aren't two different people in your mind," she told me. "That's why their voices are the same." She was right. The novel never did work. My publisher rejected it, the only time I've had a book under contract rejected in three decades of writing. The experience was sufficiently traumatic that I've forgotten even the title of that misbegotten work. All's well that ends well: the research that I did for the novel led directly to my decision five years later to write *The Making of the Atomic Bomb*. No writing is ever wasted; every sentence you write, however awkward and whether you use it or not, is a learning experience.

If you're writing verity, studying how fiction writers create and deploy characters can help you characterize real people. I tape-record interviews rather than take notes partly because a tape recorder captures the idiosyncrasies of my subject's voice. I could never invent the skateboard jockey I heard on television last night saying, "They shouldn't *downfall* skating just because of a few bad apples" and bragging of his skill that "it's not for the *meeks*." I could never invent the suburban matron I heard in a Kansas City checkout line telling her friend, of a purchase she was about to make, "That solves two birds."* My wife's two-year-old niece, Brooke, is gifted at naming; she calls an injury of any magnitude, from a scratched finger to a broken leg, an "owie" and brilliantly reduces Christmas in all its bewildering complexity to "Ho-ho." ("Who comes down the chimney?" "Ho-ho." "When do we open our presents?" "Ho-ho.") There's more to characterizing people than dialogue, but dialogue is fundamental.

For eighteen years—from 1970 until 1988—I supported myself and my family and put two children through college primarily by writing magazine articles. I still write for magazines occasionally, when I'm between books or when a magazine assignment relates to a book I'm working on and the common research solves two birds. At last count I'd published seventy-eight articles in national magazines.

Later I'll talk about the business side of magazine writing. Here I want to discuss structure.

At one time or another I've written every kind of magazine article:

* Killing two birds with one stone . . .

essay, investigation, interview, profile, experience, opinion. I had to be flexible to make a living. I wanted to be flexible to learn different ways to tell stories. How you structure an article depends partly on the material, partly on the editor and the publication. An editor may assign you an interview or a profile, possibly for a regular feature her magazine maintains. You may propose an idea that would work only as an essay/article, a form in which I specialized because I'm not brash enough to be a good investigative reporter (my kind of magazine writing is usually labeled "literary journalism"). When I was researching *The Ungodly,* I wrote an essay for *Harper's* about following the California Trail. A local collection of antique toys prompted an essay about toys and childhood for *Audience,* a hardbound magazine like a twentieth-century *American Heritage* that flared briefly in the sky back in the early 1970s and then burned out. Neither of these subjects is exactly fast-breaking news; the magazines were counting on my skill as a writer to refresh them and make them interesting.

Experiences are usually the simplest of magazine articles to write. My first assignment from *Playboy* was to travel to Ruidoso, New Mexico, and experience the annual million-dollar-stakes All-American Futurity quarter-horse race, about which I knew nothing whatsoever before I left. I went and befriended a jockey and a horse that came in second; I made notes; I returned home; I wrote "$8884.42 a Second" in one afternoon. An article for *Playboy* on a family of demolition experts in Maryland that blows up buildings for a living, "Strung Out on Blast," was similarly straightforward—I followed them around and watched them blow up an old hotel. "Germ Warfare," for *Rolling Stone,* about eradicating polio from the Western Hemisphere, took longer—I traveled with a Guatemalan public health physician to backcountry Mayan villages and attended a World Health Organization conference in Geneva—because it combined experiencing with reporting and the subject was more complex. I could have cast the story entirely as an experience: bucking through the volcano-punctuated Guatemalan mountains in a government Samurai looking for the last case of polio in all of North and South America. I could have stayed home and extracted a report from the extensive public health literature. But *Rolling Stone*'s young audience likes its information cast as adventure (so do I), so I combined the two.

I'm using "essay" a little loosely here. Magazine essays are only rarely pure essays. Usually they're essays combined with primers on the subject under discussion. In 1974, the *Atlantic* asked me to write about soybeans. The editor made it clear he didn't even know what a soybean looked like (evidently he wasn't a health food fan). The resulting essay/report, "A Bean to Feed the World," began, "A soybean is. . . ." As much as half of any article in a general-audience magazine is necessarily basic information. The structural problem you almost always face in writing such articles, then, is how to work into the story the basic information you have to supply so that readers unfamiliar with the subject know what you're talking about. You want as few seams showing as possible. I simplified the problem by developing a standard magazine voice that I try to make clear, vigorous, and authoritative. Clarity comes from careful logic and precise word choice. Sentences in the active voice with concrete verbs make vigorous prose. Authority depends on knowing the facts (or seeming to).

You can organize a magazine article rudimentarily as a sandwich: two slices of experience or reporting or essay filled with a primer on the subject under discussion. I used that structure in desperation more than once and even got by with it. More sophisticated organization requires interweaving. The best way to do that is to let your narrative determine when you stop and fill in the basics. You find something in your research that you believe readers will recognize and use that to open the story. When you come to a point that's likely to be unfamiliar, you cut away long enough to explain the context, then cut back to narrative, and so on through the article. I slip basic information (set off here in italics) into this sentence from my article

"Atomic Logic" in *Rolling Stone*, for example: "From 1945 until today, *through nearly 2,000 weapons tests worldwide and the construction of some 128,000 weapons ostensibly intended for decisive aerial, naval and ground strategic and tactical nuclear warfare,* only two nuclear weapons have ever been used in war. . . ."[2] Specialists would know those numbers; general readers probably wouldn't.

Better yet, you can fit basic information into an article organically by using it to characterize people and events. Here's a primer in diesel train controls I built into the beginning of an article I wrote for *Audience* with the deliberately gee-whiz title "How I Rode with Harold Lewis on a Diesel Freight Train Down to Gridley, Kansas, and Back." The information begins to familiarize the reader with what goes on inside the cab of a diesel train; at the same time it evidences the awesome responsibility of the locomotive engineer:

> Whether his train be merely two engines and three cars, as Harold Lewis's was when I rode back with him from Gridley, Kansas, or whether it be a monster of fourteen hundred tons, a locomotive engineer has only two controls: a throttle and a brake. Three, if you count the sander. Harold's throttle had six notches, each equivalent to approximately ten miles an hour. The brake comes in two parts, a smaller handle that controls the engine brake, a larger handle that controls the brakes on every car simultaneously. Not quite simultaneously: the air pressure feeds back from the engine a car at a time, so that each succeeding car's brake is set automatically in sequence, a matter of nice timing for the engineer as all his train work is and must be.[3]

Unlike short stories or essays, two all-at-once forms, articles have beginnings, middles, and ends. If an article is based on an experience or a report of an experience (such as a trial), those formal divisions usually correspond to the actual shape of the event. If it's based on information you've worked up, then you have to supply the structure. I went out to Oregon to look over Mount Saint Helens a year after it erupted. Tying a knot in time, I looped a compilation of eyewitness accounts of the eruption between the lines of my report on the state of the mountain and its environs now that the dust had settled. Perhaps because of its unconventional structure, perhaps because the aftermath of a volcanic eruption isn't news, the story wasn't published and earned only a kill fee (see page 151).

For a profile of Senator Edward Kennedy that I wrote back in 1971, two years after Chappaquiddick, to evoke the burden of invidious comparison it seemed to me Kennedy labored under, I began with a portentous description of a visit to the Kennedy grave site in Arlington, using a second-person variant of the indirect first-person point of view to draw the reader in:

> The cab sweeps you through Washington, past the Capitol with its braced wall and wide, empty porch, past the National Gallery where the chalk faces of the primitive dead stare from gilded frames, past the Washington Monument marble and blank and the White House twice occupied now by other men and across the bridge into the cemetery where up a hill a wooden guardhouse stands and there the driver lets you out and makes small talk with the guard and waits for you. . . .[4]

For that article, "The Last Kennedy," I read at least a dozen long books on the Kennedys and the Kennedy presidency and spent a week observing Senator Kennedy on his Washington rounds. The Kennedy family story was worn smooth by then; to give contrast to Ted Kennedy's story I had somehow to restrike it. I set up an argument—"How soon over, how soon forgotten, how soon and so narrowly entombed"—and then cut back and forth between my observation of

Ted Kennedy in the present and an allusive psychohistorical portrait of the Kennedy principals set in the past. ("The memorial in Arlington is also a family grave. The two men and the two dead children lie among soldiers' remains facing the white city. It was as a family that they presented themselves to us, or demanded that they be taken. . . .") The result looks maudlin to me at this distance, but I had identified passionately with John F. Kennedy as a young man, and the article on his younger brother was my grieving farewell.

In 1980, when the *Playboy* model and ingenue actress Dorothy Stratten was murdered by her husband, *Playboy* asked me to write an article about her. I couldn't imagine what I'd find to say about a twenty-one-year-old Playmate and hesitated to accept the assignment. But the editorial director at *Playboy*, Arthur Kretchmer, had seen me through hard times. He needed help with a story made sensitive by Hugh Hefner's fascination with Stratten, a young woman whom *Playboy* had discovered and who'd had the potential to become a major star. Understanding that Hefner would be involved and that the magazine would edit the article heavily, I reserved the right to remove my byline if I didn't like the result.

I flew to Chicago and talked with people who had known Stratten and had worked with her. I watched a videotape of her public appearances. Stratten had grown up poor in Vancouver, B.C. Her mother was a Dutch orphan who had married and emigrated to Canada to escape orphanage life. Nellie Hoogstratten was willing to talk to me. I flew to Vancouver. I had an institutional childhood and a daughter I loved, whom I couldn't imagine losing; Mrs. Hoogstratten opened up to me and I to her. She told me about her daughter's childhood, adolescence, discovery by the man who became her husband and who killed her, departure for Los Angeles. That was the interview that convinced me always to use new batteries. Mrs. Hoogstratten was skittish, and I'd let the tape recorder run in the background, afraid that she'd shy if I adjusted it. When I got to the car I discovered to my horror that the tape was inaudible. Then and there, before I drove off, I changed the batteries and dictated from memory for more than an hour.

After more interviewing, in Los Angeles, I went home to write. I found it hard to connect Mrs. Hoogstratten's radiantly innocent daughter with the glitzy vulgarity of L.A. Peter Bogdanovich, the director with whom Stratten had been living when her husband killed her, had arranged to have her buried in the same cemetery where Marilyn Monroe's mortal remains were filed in a mortuary wall and had supplied a mawkish quotation from Hemingway for Stratten's headstone. (Bogdanovich would later write a book comparing Stratten to a unicorn and marry Stratten's younger sister.) Stratten had particularly cherished playing the role of Emily in Thornton Wilder's *Our Town*. I reread Wilder's play and for the first time found myself captured by the magical resonance it sets up between the local and the universal. Emily, the ingenue of the drama, dies young in childbirth. Emily's voice was Stratten's as I found it in her diaries—"Oh, earth," Emily says finally, returning to the grave she has escaped temporarily for a rendezvous with her mother and father, "you're too wonderful for anybody to realize you. . . . Do any human beings ever realize life while they live it?" I proceeded to write a straightforward biographical profile—birth to death—in a similarly simple, direct voice, using a third-person point of view that I could shift slightly to imply internal monologue when I paraphrased Stratten from the records she left.

Structuring the story that way emphasized the pathos of Stratten's murder, much as A. E. Housman's poem "With rue my heart is laden" emphasizes the pathos of the early death of Housman's "golden friends." Unfortunately, Hefner found my version of Stratten's life too straitening. The media had attacked Hefner and his magazine for supposedly corrupting Stratten and causing her death. The attack was absurd. Stratten's husband, Paul, was a classic pimp/abuser, who murdered his wife when she refused to submit any longer to his control. But Hefner felt the need to justify himself. He took over editing the story. That it was narrated from Stratten's point of view seemingly escaped him. He'd call at midnight to quibble over a word, like a bulldog lawyer. Hefner added so much new material that the profile became the longest article *Playboy* ever published. There was nothing factual in the final result that I disagreed with, but my clear, direct narrative had been grandiloquently tycooned. I still owed Kretchmer. I compromised on a joint byline, my name "and the editors of *Playboy*."

Every magazine article is a war story. I tell these not to brag, whine, or drop names but only to demonstrate the sort of structural problems I encountered at the front. Once I did the necessary research for an article, structure almost always emerged in the struggle to write the first paragraph—not surprising, since voice and structure are united as trunk and crown. Then the story foliated, usually without complication.

The Making of the Atomic Bomb is an old-fashioned narrative history. A friend calls it "your eighteenth-century book." It flirts briefly with implied internal monologue in the first chapter, tracking Leo Szilard across the fateful Southampton Row intersection where he conceived of a nuclear chain reaction. Thereafter it settles down to straightforward third-person omniscient narration. Deciding on a voice was the easy part.

Structure was less obvious. I had a nearly overwhelming quantity of information to organize. Organization took the form of parallel chronologies: the development of nuclear physics and its consequent technology, the lulls and riots of international politics, the biographies of several dozen exceptional scientists, the monstrous twentieth-century elaboration of manmade death. I couldn't tell all these stories simultaneously. I couldn't run them side by side, since the narrative line of a book is always a unitary line. (Most experimental writing is an attempt to defeat the linear organization of written language. James Joyce, for example, was trying to run multiple narratives on the same line when he invented portmanteau words—suitcase words that punned two or more words together—for *Finnegans Wake.* Overlap made Joyce's prose hard to understand, just as it does when several people at once try to talk.) So I decided to arrange the several stories in interrupted narrative segments, one and then the next and the next and the next and then back to the first, starting where I'd left off earlier. That's how the phone company transmits multiple conversations on the same line. Sometimes, to reach a logical stopping point, I had to carry one segment of narrative farther forward in time than the previous segment had moved. When I cycled back to the previous segment, I usually summarized to catch up.

This organization made demands on the reader, who has to hold several narratives simultaneously in her head. In exchange, she gets scale and connection. *The Making of the Atomic Bomb* is in fact four or five books in one, which is why it's so long. The alternating parallel narratives clarify historical relationships. Halting one narrative to shift to another sets up the book as a series of cliff-hangers, fitting Dostoyevsky's shrewd dramatic rule—which he learned the hard way, knocking out books chapter by chapter as newspaper serials—that a writer should end every chapter with either a door slammed shut or a door flung open.

Not everyone liked the arrangement. Dixie Lee Ray, the eccentric former chair of the U.S. Atomic Energy Commission and governor of the state of Washington, reviewed *The Making of the Atomic Bomb* for the *Washington Times.* My war scenes were too graphic, Dr. Ray complained. Everyone knows that war is terrible; why go on about it? Worse, she wrote, the book *jumps around.*

Although I'd read through all my research material once, I knew I'd have to work through it again minutely as I wrote. Each chapter would require reviewing hundreds of documents and dozens of books. Sometimes I had to retrieve the books from the library and even through interlibrary loan, which limited how long I could hold them. I didn't see how I could write a draft of the entire book straight through, as writers normally do, and then proceed to successive book-length drafts as I edited. Instead I decided to finish each chapter to the fine-sanding stage before hewing out the next. I could do that because I had organized my several chronologies sufficiently to know where I was going. I shaped each long chapter around significant events.

Characters gave me another kind of structural continuity. Leo Szilard happened to have been present at most of the significant turning points of the early atomic age. He grew up in Hungary, whence a core group of émigré scientists came who started the United States government thinking about an atomic bomb; he escaped Nazi Germany; he conceived of a nuclear chain reaction; he emigrated to the United States; he conducted one of the first experiments that revealed that fissioning uranium released enough secondary neutrons to sustain a chain reaction; he coinvented the nuclear reactor with Enrico Fermi; he helped design and build the first nuclear reactor; he gave early thought to the consequences of the atomic bomb. Szilard was a clothesline upon which I could hang the story. So was the Danish physicist Niels Bohr, who came and went less frequently but whose appearances provided moments when I could examine with him the profound changes that the discovery of nuclear fission would bring to international politics.

A less global structural problem was deciding at what level to pitch scientific explanation. I'd read enough popular science to be impatient with explanation that depended on fanciful analogies. Besides being condescending, comparing an atom to a watermelon wastes half the analogy. Fortunately, nuclear physics is largely an experimental science. Reading through some of the classic papers in the field, I realized that I could explain a result clearly and simply by describing the physical experiment that produced it: a brass box, the air evacuated, a source of radiation in the box in the form of a vial of radon gas, and so on. Then I and the reader could visualize a process in terms of the manipulation of real laboratory objects, not watermelons, just as the experimenters themselves did, and could absorb the culture of scientific work at the same time—the throb of the vacuum pump, the smell of its oil.

I made a basic rule that I would look up and explain anything I didn't know about. I'm reasonably well educated; if I didn't know, I assumed many readers wouldn't know either. When I came to the Jewish emigration from the Russian Pale of Settlement into central Europe and the West, I realized I'd never understood how the Jews got from Roman Palestine to Czarist Russia in the first place. That's why there's a capsule history of the Diaspora in a book on the atomic bomb.

Finally, as I mentioned earlier, I decided to tell the story as much as possible in the words of those who experienced it. I had the great advantage that the several hundred scientists who lived the development of nuclear physics and its military application counted among the most intelligent, articulate, and interesting men and women of the twentieth century. Many of them had written memoirs or given oral histories. Often I found myself in the enviable position of having to choose from three or four accurate, colorful, but differently phrased versions of the same anecdote. Sources don't come much richer than that.

Hard and sometimes frustrating work that it is, writing leads to communication and connection. After *The Making of the Atomic Bomb* was published, the physics community accepted me into its company as a sort of minor poet laureate. I spoke to the Harvard physics faculty; I spoke at the fiftieth anniversary of the first controlled nuclear chain reaction; I spoke at the fiftieth reunion of the Los Alamos veterans and pioneers. If I'd ever felt I lacked one, the older generation of physicists gave me a community to call my own. I continue to earn royalties from *The Making of the Atomic Bomb,* which I value, but I value beyond measure the appreciation of people whose work, I believe, forced an end to world-scale war.

Seven

EDITING

Editing isn't a cosmetic process. It's a thinking process. Expression usually emerges from the preconscious mind only loosely organized. Images body forth; memories, ideas, associations, tumble onto the page. The hound dog of memory that you send out for language retrieves the first quarry it finds in the quarter where you aimed it. Sometimes it offers up the right word, sometimes it offers up a remote third cousin, sometimes a dead fish. Not to decorate an infelicitous choice, not to "use the active voice" or to obey other stylistic edicts but to make as clear as you can, to yourself and to your reader, what you "mean," you have to edit.

What does it mean to "mean"? "You know what I *meant* to say," a student asserts petulantly, defending a paper, "even if I didn't use the right words." It's true, you do, more often than not, if you're familiar with the context, if you're feeling charitable, if you give this word choice and that word choice the benefit of the doubt. Language is sufficiently redundant to make it possible, barely, to know what someone "meant" to say even if he didn't use the "right words." He used other words, which collectively allowed some approximation of his "meaning." This possibility implies that "meaning" is somehow preverbal. Ultimately, it may be, but proximately, meaning is distributed among the many redundant ways of saying something. And that's the challenge of editing. You can't ever say *only* what you mean. You always say *more* as well. The purpose of editing is to localize and fix your meaning more precisely—for yourself first of all and then for your reader. The purpose of editing is to make as certain as humanly possible that the *more* you always say also says what you mean.

If you mean to say a house, do you mean a Masai house of sticks plastered with cow manure, or a European house of brick, or an American house of wood? They will equally be houses, but each will be more as well. A physicist who escaped to the United States from Nazi Germany in the 1930s was disturbed, on the train from New York City to Princeton, to see all the wooden houses—in Europe, he writes, wooden houses "are looked down upon as cheap substitutes which do not, like brick, resist the attack of passing time." In Princeton on a Saturday afternoon, the physicist found the streets empty of students. He inquired at his hotel where all the students had gone. Perhaps to see Notre Dame, the clerk told him. "Was I crazy?" the physicist asked himself. "Notre Dame is in Paris. Here is Princeton with its empty streets. What does it all mean?" Then the Princeton–Notre Dame football game ended, "cars began to run, crowds of people streamed through the streets, noisy students shouted and sang."[1] How could the physicist know what it all "meant"? He didn't know why Americans build wooden houses—because wood is plentiful here—and the clerk didn't supply the context necessary to differentiate Notre Dame Cathedral in Paris from the University of Notre Dame, or explain that "to see Notre Dame" was a metonym for "to see Princeton University play the University of Notre Dame in football."

Worse yet, if you don't say what you mean, your reader will say it for you, willy-nilly. When I see an incoherent film I usually complain about its incoherence. That surprises my friends, who proceed to explain to me what isn't in the script. They write their own stories to fill in what's missing. Hollywood, with its contempt for the people who make it rich, expects no less of us: ya got spectacle, ya got stars, ya want *coherence*? Filling in gaps is the way our facile brains work. There's a blind spot in the eye, but you'll never see it unless you make special arrangements to look—the brain fills it in. Give people random sequences of numbers or other symbols and they'll usually find a pattern that isn't there. But you don't want people to write *their* stories into your work, to find patterns that aren't there. You want people to read *your* stories, to find the patterns you designed.

Words are always approximate. Even if you and I agree on the definition of a word, even if we know its official history, it also has private associations for each of us that shade it differently. "The social work office where I was employed," writes Sallie Tisdale in her memoir, *Talk Dirty to Me*, "held a seminar on sexuality." One exercise, "a homework assignment," required the participants "to make a collage that expressed our own sexuality." Well, sexuality. That ought to be obvious. It wasn't. "The next morning I saw that my colleagues, male and female both, had all made romantic visions of candlelight and sunsets. Then I presented my own, a vision of masked men and women, naked torsos, skin everywhere, darkness, heat. . . . I didn't expect or quite understand the ringing silence with which my collage was met."[2]

Context can prevent confusion, but entrenched private meanings may be lodged beyond a writer's control (if a reader is phobic about snakes, you probably aren't going to decondition her in the space of a page). Readers are less tolerant of vagueness. The student who knew what he meant probably knew vaguely. I knew vaguely what I meant when I started working, in the previous chapter, on the sentence (about Hugh Hefner's editing of my profile of Dorothy Stratten) that in final form became "There was nothing factual in the final result that I disagreed with, but my clear, direct narrative had been grandiloquently tycooned." Most of the sentence emerged on first draft. "Di-

rect" was originally "simple." I rejected "simple" first because it implied that my problem with Hefner's editing might have been its complexity rather than its verbosity. "Simple" also has connotations of "simpleminded," which I certainly didn't want to volunteer to characterize my work. Finally, "clear" and "simple" seemed too much alike, blurring the distinction I was trying to make rather than drawing it; "clear" and "direct" complement each other.

I had to work to get "grandiloquently tycooned," however. I knew I wanted a striking phrase to sum up the story. I knew I wanted the phrase to echo what I'd written earlier about finding it hard to connect "radiantly innocent" Stratten with the "glitzy vulgarity" of Los Angeles.* What came to mind first of all was a pun: "malled" for "mauled" (i.e., "my . . . narrative had been malled"). L.A., the automobile, shopping malls: malled. But except for their physical proximity as common occupants of the Los Angeles basin, malls and Hefner have nothing in common—the man's a recluse and someone else does his shopping.

So then:

developed / real estate / gentrified / monstrosity [?]
malled and multinationaled

Then something in "multinationaled" recalled to me my experience over the years with various self-made million- and billionaires, all of whom have been (not to put too fine a point on it) eccentric, and that personification of the meaning I was looking for called up:

tycooned and multinationaled

* Speaking of private meanings, I didn't realize until now, going over the work, the extent to which I was setting up a proportion: Stratten: L.A. = Rhodes Stratten draft: Hefner's editing. No wonder I drafted "simple" instead of "direct"—I was thinking of Stratten.

And as soon as I typed "tycoon" (from Japanese *taikun,* "great lord or prince," but comically echoing "raccoon," an unrelated word from Algonquian, because of the rhyme and the little animal's bandit mask and thievish reputation), I knew I had the right word and now needed only to find an appropriate adjective to modify it, so a stab in the dark:

egregiously tycooned

Then I looked up "egregious"—literally, "towering above the flock," with a modern ironic sense of "gross, flagrant, outrageous." That wasn't what I wanted, either literally or ironically. I wanted something comic, not hostile; Hefner meant me no harm. So:

immoderate/ intemperate/ large

which led to "grandiose," and just down the road on the same screen of my electronic dictionary was "grandiloquent," great-speaking, characterized by swelling or pompous expression. It was expression I was talking about, Hefner editing my draft. So: "grandiloquently tycooned." I could have written "badly edited" and saved myself a lot of work, but what would you have taken home from that?

Worse vagueness is writing around words you don't know. I spent hours one day trying to look up the name for the little indentation on the upper lip. I didn't have an anatomy text (I do now). I finally found the word: sulcus. (Technically, *sulcus nasolabialis;* there are many sulci—grooves and furrows—on and in the body.) If I'd written "the little indentation on the upper lip" you'd have known what I meant and you'd also know that I didn't know its name. "Sulcus" is sufficiently obscure that you might have forgiven me. On the other hand, if he doesn't know the name for part of his own face, what else doesn't he know? Can I trust what he says here? And even if your

reader lets you off the hook, you've distracted her from the virtual reality you're trying to project, she's caught on to your hocus-pocus, she's paying attention to the man behind the curtain, whom you want her to ignore.

To demonstrate editing for writing, I'm going to compose a brief text here and now from beginning to end and try to explain my choices as I go along. I haven't prepared even a subject or a theme. It ought to be something that relates to the subject of this book, so that you won't be wasting your time comparing an atom to a watermelon. Let's see. It would be fun if it were halfway humorous. How about reference books? Okay. Here we go. I'll change the typeface to set off the composition from my running narrative and use slashes to indicate restarts.

> Any good book / Many books on writing / The library is full of references. / The library is full of reference books. / There's a roomful of reference books at the library. (I'm feeling self-conscious here. Bear with me; I'll get over it.) Reference books. Any public library is one vast reference book. I go there when all else fails, but it's nice / I like to / but I keep a / Any public library is one vast reference book, / The public library is one vast reference book, a treasure (I'm checking the thesaurus for a fresher word) vault / fortune / stockpile / cache / wealth / abundance / profusion / an abundance. (Now I'm going to look up "abundance" to see what its roots are; they're elegant: "abundant" comes from words meaning to flow in waves, an overflowing of liquid.) (Now let's start over with a fresh copy:)
>
> Reference books. The public library is one vast reference book, an abundance (but I couldn't see where to go from

there, and as I sat stewing, "abundance" reminded me of "bounty," and "bounty" suggested "harvest," which flashed a quick visual association with a grain bin—the public library as a grain bin filled with a harvest that sustains us; but before I go on I'm going to look up "bounty": curious, it's from the Latin for "goodness," related to "bonus," and emerges from an Indo-European root signifying "to do, to perform, show favor, revere"). The public library is a grain bin / is a harvest bountiful with grain / You can scoop facts by the shovel load from the grain bin of the public library, but it's nice to keep an emergency kit / emergency supply / emergency store at home. (I used to shovel corn from a bin at the boys' home with a scoop shovel, a balanced, leveraged instrument, its scoop broad and belled as a tractor seat.) (Cleaning up once more:)

Reference books. You can scoop facts by the shovel load from the grain bin of the public library, but it's nice / useful to keep an emergency store at home. Dictionaries I've already discussed (I got the *OED* on CD-ROM for my birthday last week!). The one-volume *Columbia Encyclopedia* is invaluable. When I was writing *The Making of the Atomic Bomb* I acquired a used set / a set of used volumes of the *Encyclopaedia Britannica*. Unfortunately, it was an edition that had been only intermittently / fragmentarily / partially updated since the end of the Second World War and contained / included few references to the scientists I was writing about, many of whom came to prominence as a result of their war work. A new edition of the *EB* would be valuable / helpful / useful, but it's expensive. I stick with / content myself with *The Columbia Encyclopedia* and count on my extensive collection of books / turn to my personal library, accumulated catch-as-catch-can / randomly (thesaurus time; yes:) / haphazardly over the years, for fines that escape its screen ("fines," not penalties but a technical term for finely ground grain, may be too obscure; ah, here's a context to define it:) / the fines that fall through its screen. (And the image continues the grain/bounty imagery that framed this discussion.) (This feels like a paragraph break—the paragraph is getting long and I'm ready to switch to discussing another reference.)

Less obvious references that I find useful include *The Macmillan Visual Dictionary,* which pictures thousands of objects and labels their parts (but called a shovel a shovel without confirming / called a shovel a shovel when I looked it up a moment ago / a minute ago without naming its carrying part); a medical dictionary; a dictionary of science; the *Merck Manual* and the *Merck Veterinary Manual* for human and veterinary diseases; an anatomy text; foreign-language dictionaries (I have German, French, Latin, and for some reason Polish); biographical dictionaries such as *Makers of Nineteenth Century Culture* and *20th Century Culture;* and any technical manuals and handbooks you come across / you happen to acquire. I have several collections of aphorisms I don't think / that I don't think I've ever consulted—*Bartlett's* seems to do the job / seems to be adequate for my needs, especially now that Justin Kaplan has pulled away all the layers of lace and velvet curtains that blocked the / blocked its light. / pulled down the dusty drapes / draping (I'm thinking about the draping on nineteenth-century coffins but don't know what that form of decoration was called; the material was crepe; bunting? to the *OED* again; no, bunting is flag material; but crepe has possibilities) / has pulled down the dusty crepe that blocked its light. (But now I've gone too far and lost the connection with the "ceremonial boilerplate" and "gassy platitudes" that Kaplan removed from the edition he edited. Let's see:)

Bartlett's seems to be adequate for my needs, especially now that Justin Kaplan has pulled down the layers of lace and dusty crepe that blocked its light. (I'd like to have used the word "drapes," but "drape" nearly rhymes with "crepe"—"drapes of dusty crepe" would stop a reader with a sensitive ear—and I want to keep that allusion to death and, by extension, dead language. "Pulled down" serves to imply drapes, as does the fact that the "layers" of material blocked the light.) (Let's recopy this second paragraph once more before we go on:)

Less obvious references that I find useful include *The Macmillan Visual Dictionary,* which pictures thousands of objects and labels their parts (but called a shovel a shovel when I looked it up a minute ago without naming its carrying part); a medical dictionary; a dictionary of science; the *Merck Manual* and the *Merck Veterinary Manual* for human and veterinary diseases; an anatomy text; foreign-language dictionaries (I have German, French, Latin, and for some reason Polish); biographical dictionaries such as *Makers of Nineteenth Century Culture* and *20th Century Culture;* and any technical manuals and handbooks that happen to turn up. I have several collections of aphorisms that I don't think I've ever consulted—*Bartlett's* seems to be adequate for my needs, especially now that Justin Kaplan has pulled down the layers of lace and dusty crepe that blocked its light.

(But damn, I see the connection still isn't clear. I need some more direct allusion to words:) *Bartlett's* seems to be adequate for my needs, especially now that Justin Kaplan has pulled down the layers of fustian (wait—what's fustian? To the *OED:* "a thick, twilled, cotton cloth with a short pile or nap, usually dyed of an olive, leaden, or other dark colour";

with its overtones of "fussy" and its literary usage as a pejorative for ornate writing, that's what I want) and dusty boilerplate (borrowing Kaplan's word, which commonly refers to stereotyped writing and which is surprising in this context) that blocked its light. (There. Whew.) (Paragraph time again.)

I have an economics textbook that I've never used. I've never consulted *The Timetables of History*. I use an atlas all the time, most recently to locate obscure towns in Russia / in the former Soviet Union so that I can locate them for readers by reference to the nearest familiar Soviet cities in my / so that I could locate them for readers in my book *Dark Sun*.

And then there are the sweet-spot books / And then I have my secret weapons. I have four secret weapons. One is a collection / a 64-page collection of selections / a 64-page assortment of selections ("collection of selections" calls attention to itself for no good reason; "assortment," with its slightly comic suggestion of an assortment of hard candies, is just right) from the writings of Ralph Waldo Emerson, a writer far less saccharine / the world's best aphorist, a far less saccharine writer than (but Emerson's not merely *less* saccharine) / not at all the saccharine writer many Americans think / believe / imagine. Here's an example, to catch the flavor ("flavor" carrying on the candy metaphor, as, by contrast, does the word "saccharine"), which ought / one I often use as an after-dinner speaker at banquets, which ought to send a shiver up your spine:

> Nature is no sentimentalist—does not cosset or pamper us. We must see that the world is rough and surly, and will not mind drowning a man or a woman, but swallows your ship like a grain of dust.... The way of Providence is a little rude. The habit of snake and spi-

> der, the snap of the tiger and other leapers and bloody jumpers, the crackle of the bones of his prey in the coil of the anaconda—these are in the system, and our habits are like theirs. (Now comes the part that shivers banquet guests:) You have just dined, and however scrupulously the slaughter-house is concealed in the graceful distance of miles, there is complicity, expensive races—race living at the expense of race. . . .

Another secret weapon is *Le Mot Juste,* a dictionary of classical and foreign words and phrases. Only the most urbane writers have Greek, Latin, French, German, Italian, Spanish, and what the dictionary terms "miscellaneous languages" at their fingertips. I'm the least urbane of writers. When the *New York Review of Books* lays a French phrase on me that any private-school twit ought to / would know, I confer with / refer to *Le Mot Juste* and find "the right word." It's good for browsing, too, to load your quiver with darts / to reload your / It's a source as well as a reference, darts for your quiver.

Secret weapons three and four are affiliate. (I like the sound of that, but I'm not sure it's quite right; the *OED* says it means "received into intimate connection"; let's try the thesaurus: allied, associated; okay, I'll stay with "affiliate" for now.) One is *The Baby Name Book,* which supplies me with a range of first names for characters / with a list of first names for characters that includes the names' meanings / which lists first names / which lists and explains first names / a 99-cent special sold at supermarket checkouts. It lists first names with their national origins and meanings. / It lists first names, boys and girls both, with national origin and meaning ("Eric—'ruler' "; "Rachel—'innocent one' "). I use it for naming / to name characters. The other / The fourth and last is a modest collection of small-town phone books. They supply last names for characters. For some reason, big-city phone books don't have the range I'm looking for / Big-city phone books, even though they include tens of thousands more names, don't serve as well. Small towns seem to have kept the old, odd names going. Something in the water, or maybe it's inbreeding.

(I could end there, and perhaps I should, but I'd like to see if I can find a line or two for all the electronic databases people celebrate these days. So, new paragraph:) My daughter tells me (I just got off the phone—she called to ask me to send her one of my books to give as a gift, and the subject happened to come up) she / her lab / she and her colleagues find their references on-line these days and no longer use a / consult a CD-ROM that used to come monthly by subscription. They're not trying to write. / They're only sequencing DNA; they're not trying to write. I'd rather have my reference books about me. That's not an antiquarian fancy. It takes forever to call up an on-line database, and while your knowbot is bursting through successive screens into the glory vault like (I have an image in my head, but I can't quite place it, something astronautical) / is bursting through successive screens like the *Enterprise* (but I don't quite know what they call it on *Star Trek,* so I'd better not risk calling down the wrath of the Trekkies; it's not important enough to go to all the trouble of looking up) / like a starship bursting through hyperspace, you're sitting at your computer desk twiddling your thumbs. Wonderful as computers are for word processing, they're still not much larger than keyholes / they're still / they're hardly more than keyholes / their view of the larger world is hardly more than a keyhole / they allow only a keyhole view of the world. No one ever invented a better piece of hardware than a book. / a more efficient, user-friendly / a friendlier ("user-friendly" will sound like the awkward fad word it is in a few months or years; it's better to stick to standard English unless you're talking about slang usage) / No one ever invented a friendlier data storage device than a book.

(So. Good enough. Now let's pull the whole thing together and go over it once more for fine-tuning:)

Reference books. You can scoop facts by the shovel load from the grain bin (I don't need "grain"; "scoop" and "bin" carry the figure without the more literal "grain") / from the generous bins (my first thought was "bountiful bins," but I don't like the gratuitous alliteration) of the public library, but it's useful to keep an emergency store at home. Dictionaries I've already discussed (I got the *OED* on CD-ROM for my birthday last week!). The one-volume (I use the word "volume" again in the next sentence; it's unnecessary here) / *The Columbia Encyclopedia* is invaluable. When I was writing *The Making of the Atomic Bomb* I acquired a set of used volumes of the *Encyclopaedia Britannica*. (What is it I acquired here? Why "acquired"? Why not "bought"? "Old words are best," Winston Churchill once said; "old words when short are best of all.") / I bought a set of the *Encyclopaedia Britannica*. Unfortunately, it was an edition (but "it" doesn't work with "set") / Unfortunately, the edition had been only partially (wrong word) / partly updated since the end of the Second World War and included few references to the scientists I was writing about, many of whom came to prominence as a result of their war work. A new edition of the *EB* would be useful to have, ("to have" added since the previous draft, to be more specific) but it's expensive. I content myself with the

Columbia Encyclopedia and turn to my personal library, accumulated haphazardly over the years (do I need "over the years"? No: "accumulated" carries that sense) / accumulated haphazardly (but I think I'll reverse the sequence of these two words, for logic and emphasis, to put the verb at the end) / haphazardly accumulated, for fines that fall through its screen. ("its" is a problem. The most annoying, and often the most intractable, problems of editing are pronoun problems. I'm constantly fiddling with antecedents when I edit. Here "its" refers grammatically to "my personal library" when it ought to refer to *The Columbia Encyclopedia.* So I'll have to fix it. Oh, I see; not so hard) / for fines (and let's explain this obscure word's venue) / for fines of information that fall through the *Encyclopedia*'s screen / coarse screen.

Less obvious references that I find useful include *The Macmillan Visual Dictionary,* which pictures thousands of objects and labels their parts (but called a shovel a shovel when I looked it up a minute ago without naming its carrying part) (do I need this rather obscure complaint in the midst of an already complicated list? I don't think I do; if I wanted to keep it, I'd have to rewrite it and fix that faulty final phrase "without naming its carrying part," which seems to refer to my action looking up the word "shovel" rather than to a failing of the dictionary) / and labels their parts; a medical dictionary; a dictionary of science; the *Merck Manual* and the *Merck Veterinary Manual* for human and veterinary diseases; an anatomy text; foreign-language dictionaries (I have German, French, Latin, and for some reason Polish); biographical dictionaries such as *Makers of Nineteenth Century Culture* and *20th Century Culture;* and any technical manuals and handbooks that happen to turn up. I have several collections of aphorisms that I don't think I've ever consulted—*Bartlett's* seems to be adequate for my needs, especially now that Justin Kaplan (but not everyone will know who Kaplan is and what he's done, so I'll add a brief explanation) in the revised 16th edition (I started to write "in the new 16th edition," but it won't be new if this little book of mine stays in print a few years; "revised" does the job without dating the reference) has pulled down the layers of fustian and dusty boilerplate that blocked its light. ("Fust-" and "dust-" rhyme, but in this case it's sufficiently quiet that it works.)

I have an economics textbook that I've never used. I've never consulted *The Timetables of History*. I use an atlas all the time (uh-oh: *Timetables* and "time" echo each other; if I let that repetition get through, readers would fairly accuse me of nodding) / I use an atlas often—most recently to locate obscure towns in the former Soviet Union so that I could locate (same problem: "locate" twice in the same sentence) / most recently to identify obscure towns in the former Soviet Union so that I could locate them for readers in my book *Dark Sun*.

And then I have my secret weapons. I have four secret weapons. One is a 64-page assortment of selections from the writings of Ralph Waldo Emerson, the world's best aphorist, not at all the saccharine writer many Americans imagine (I still don't like "imagine." To the thesaurus. Ah:) / many Americans scorn. Here's an example, to catch the flavor (example of what?) / Here's an example of Emerson's grit (but grit doesn't have a "flavor," so I'll have to give up the phrase "to catch the flavor," even though "flavor" carries along the subterranean metaphor of a candy assortment; I'll give it up because I like "grit" better) / of Emerson's grit, one I often use as an after-dinner speaker at banquets (where else would an after-dinner speaker speak? at home to his family, thumbs hooked into his galluses?) / one I often use as an after-dinner speaker, which ought to send a shiver up your spine:

> Nature is no sentimentalist—does not cosset or pamper us. We must see that the world is rough and surly, and will not mind drowning a man or a woman, but swallows your ship like a grain of dust.... The way of Providence is a little rude. The habit of snake and spider, the snap of the tiger and other leapers and bloody jumpers, the crackle of the bones of his prey in the coil of the anaconda—these are in the system, and our habits are like theirs. You have just dined, and however scrupulously the slaughter-house is concealed in the graceful distance of miles, there is complicity, expensive races—race living at the expense of race....

Another secret weapon is *Le Mot Juste,* a dictionary of classical and foreign words and phrases. Only the most urbane writers have Greek, Latin, French, German, Italian, Spanish, and what the dictionary terms "miscellaneous languages" at their fingertips. I'm the least urbane of writers. When the *New York Review of Books* lays a French phrase on me (you understand that I'm using this dated slang ironically to mock the arrogance of intellectuals who assume in the late twentieth century that everyone who's anyone knows French, a marginal language still forced on children in private schools who would be better off learning Japanese) that any private-school twit would know, I refer to *Le Mot Juste* and find "the right word." It's a source as well as a reference, darts for your quiver. (Quivers hold arrows; do they also hold darts? Anyway, I don't like ending a sentence, much less a paragraph, on a rising inflection. Let's see:) / It's a source as well as a reference; sometimes only a foreign word or phrase will serve.

Secret weapons three and four are affiliate. One is *The Baby Name Book*, a 99-cent special sold at supermarket checkouts. It lists first names of ("of" added) boys and girls both, with national origin and meaning / with their national origins and meanings ("Eric—'ruler'"; "Rachel—'innocent one'"). I use it to name / to christen my characters. The fourth and last is a modest collection of / Finally, the fourth and last secret weapon / A modest collection of small-town phone books is the last secret weapon (adding:)—for family names. (deleting:) ~~They supply last names for characters.~~ / Big-city phone books, even though they include tens of thousands more names, don't serve as well. Small towns seem to have kept the old, odd names going. Something in the water, or maybe it's inbreeding. (But the end of this paragraph needs reworking. "Inbreeding" is an old and ignorant joke. The real conclusion is the sentence about big-city phone books. So I'll work things around:) / Small towns have kept up the old, odd names. Big-city phone books, even with their crowds, don't serve as well.

My daughter tells me she and her colleagues find their references on-line these days and no longer consult a CD-ROM that used to come monthly by subscription. They're only sequencing DNA; they're not trying to write. I'd rather have my reference books about me. That's not an antiquarian fancy. It takes forever to call up an on-line database, and while your knowbot is bursting through successive screens like a starship bursting ("bursting" twice makes the comparison too loud, I think, so:) / like a starship maneuvering through hyperspace, you're sitting at your computer desk (too descriptive; it kills the joke) / you're sitting twiddling your thumbs. Wonderful as computers are for word processing, they allow only a keyhole view of the world. No one ever invented a friendlier data storage device than a book.

(Let's copy it out once more, for one final review:)
Reference books. You can scoop facts by the shovel load from the generous bins of the public library, but it's useful to keep an emergency store at home. Dictionaries I've already discussed (I got the *OED* on CD-ROM for my birthday last week!). *The Columbia Encyclopedia* is invaluable. When I was writing *The Making of the Atomic Bomb* I acquired a set of used volumes of the *Encyclopaedia Britannica*. Unfortunately, the edition had been only partly updated since the end of the Second World War and included few references to the scientists I was writing about, many of whom came to prominence as a result of their war work. A new edition of the *EB* would be useful to have, but it's expensive. I content myself with *The Columbia Encyclopedia* and turn to my personal library, haphazardly accumulated, for fines of information that fall through the *Encyclopedia*'s coarse screen.

Less obvious references that I find useful include *The Macmillan Visual Dictionary,* which pictures thousands of objects and labels their parts; a medical dictionary; a dictionary of science; the *Merck Manual* and the *Merck Veterinary Manual* for human and veterinary diseases; an anatomy text; foreign-language dictionaries (I have German, French, Latin, and for some reason Polish); biographical dictionaries such as *Makers of Nineteenth Century Culture* and *20th Century Culture;* and any technical manuals and handbooks that happen to turn up. I have several collections of aphorisms that I don't think I've ever consulted—*Bartlett's* seems to be adequate for my needs, especially now that Justin Kaplan in the revised 16th edition has pulled down the layers of fustian and dusty boilerplate that blocked its light.

I have an economics textbook that I've never used. I've never consulted *The Timetables of History*. I use an atlas often—most recently to identify obscure towns in the former Soviet Union so that I could locate them for readers in my book *Dark Sun*.

And then I have my secret weapons. I have four secret weapons. One is a 64-page assortment of selections from the writings of Ralph Waldo Emerson, the world's best aphorist, not at all the saccharine writer many Americans scorn. Here's an example of Emerson's grit, one I often use as an after-dinner speaker, which ought to send a shiver up your spine:

> Nature is no sentimentalist—does not cosset or pamper us. We must see that the world is rough and surly, and will not mind drowning a man or a woman, but swallows your ship like a grain of dust.... The way of Providence is a little rude. The habit of snake and spider, the snap of the tiger and other leapers and bloody jumpers, the crackle of the bones of his prey in the coil of the anaconda—these are in the system, and our habits are like theirs. You have just dined, and however scrupulously the slaughter-house is concealed in the graceful distance of miles, there is complicity, expensive races—race living at the expense of race....

Another secret weapon is *Le Mot Juste,* a dictionary of classical and foreign words and phrases. Only the most urbane writers have Greek, Latin, French, German, Italian,

Spanish, and what the dictionary terms "miscellaneous languages" at their fingertips. I'm the least urbane of writers. When the *New York Review of Books* lays a French phrase on me that any private-school twit would know, I refer to *Le Mot Juste* and find "the right word." It's a source as well as a reference; sometimes only a foreign word or phrase will do.

Secret weapons three and four are affiliate. One is *The Baby Name Book,* a 99-cent special sold at supermarket checkouts. It lists first names of boys and girls with their national origins and meanings ("Eric—'ruler'"; "Rachel—'innocent one'"). I use it to christen my characters. A modest collection of small-town phone books is the last secret weapon—for family names. Small towns have kept up the old, odd names. Big-city phone books, even with their crowds, don't serve as well.

My daughter tells me she and her colleagues find their references on-line these days and no longer consult a CD-ROM that used to come monthly by subscription. They're only sequencing DNA; they're not trying to write. I'd rather have my reference books about me. That's not an antiquarian fancy. It takes forever to call up an on-line database, and while your knowbot is bursting through successive screens like a starship maneuvering through hyperspace, you're sitting twiddling your thumbs. Wonderful as computers are for word processing, they allow only a keyhole view of the world. No one ever invented a friendlier data storage device than a book.

Because the essay is a casual form, and one I've had years of practice writing, I was able to outline this modest work mentally as I went along and draft and edit concurrently. With less experience, or writing to a more exacting form, you may find it easier to proceed sequentially, making notes first, then drafting, then editing.

There are other kinds of editing besides the editing I've demonstrated writing this brief essay. Scientific and historical writing require much more careful attention to formal logic; fiction needs to be reviewed for fidelity to voice and point of view. Nor is editing ever really finished. Every sentence might be further improved, although it's also true that work can be overedited. The problem arises most acutely in the sentences embodying figures of speech, the very sentences on which I worked hardest in the drafting process you just followed with me. You can crank metaphors up only so tight before they begin to sound forced. The best editors I've worked with had what seemed to me an uncanny ability to single out for revision precisely those sentences I'd worked hardest to perfect. My editors may not have been psychic; they may simply have been alert to purple prose. James Dickey once wrote that he needed about one hundred fifty drafts of a poem to get it right and fifty more to make it sound spontaneous.

As you may have noticed following my editing example, you reach a point in editing where the words lie dead on the page, no longer evoking much emotional response as you reread them. Sometimes, proofreading a set of book galleys, I've found myself reading along thinking of something else entirely, my daydream strewing uncaught typos in its wake. When writing goes dead you need to put it away for a while. If you're writing against a deadline, you simply have to shake your head to clear away the cobwebs and focus your attention more closely on the words you've allowed familiarity to blur.

Because it's possible for those helpful strangers called editors to rework a piece of writing, people think of editing as somehow detachable—a separate, rational, Apollonian procedure worked upon the irrational, Dionysian creative draft. Editing is in fact simply *more writ-*

ing—a higher-level (or lower-level, if you prefer) version of the same process whereby you produced the creative draft in the first place. It's certainly not purely rational, nor is it more rational than creative drafting. You think at every stage when you write; you don't only feel. You wrestle with words at every stage, because writing is made of words. Editing operates on a different level from creative drafting because it takes as its ground the words on the page rather than the preverbal collectivities that preceded them. But it's equally a part of the creative process.

When editors rewrite your work, the work becomes collective. It's no longer entirely yours. I understood when I became a professional writer that writing articles for magazines would be a collective process. Magazine editors tell me they edit my work less than most. If so, that's because I write with a magazine's audience and house style very much in mind. At the same time, I decided that I would fiercely resist allowing anyone to rewrite my books. I welcome corrections of lapses of grammar and misused words. I'm willing to cut if length is a problem, as it was with *The Making of the Atomic Bomb.* (I turned in a manuscript of fifteen hundred pages, which would have necessitated publishing it as a two-volume work; instead my editor and I cut it to a thousand manuscript pages and published it as one volume thick enough to serve as a makeshift high chair for Thanksgiving dinner.) But my books are mine, my work, with my name on them, and I edit them myself.

ing—a higher-level (or lower-level, if you prefer) version of the same process whereby you produced the creative draft in the first place. It's certainly not purely rational, nor is it more rational than creative drafting. You think at every stage when you write; you don't only feel. You wrestle with words at every stage, because writing is made of words. Editing operates on a different level from creative drafting because it takes as its ground the words on the page rather than the preverbal collectivities that preceded them. But it's equally a part of the creative process.

When editors rewrite your work, the work becomes collective. It's no longer entirely yours. I understood when I became a professional writer that writing articles for magazines would be a collective process. Magazine editors tell me they edit my work less than most. If so, that's because I write with a magazine's audience and house style very much in mind. At the same time, I decided that I would fiercely resist allowing anyone to rewrite my books. I welcome corrections of lapses of grammar and misused words. I'm willing to cut if length is a problem, as it was with *The Making of the Atomic Bomb*. (I turned in a manuscript of fifteen hundred pages, which would have necessitated publishing it as a two-volume work; instead my editor and I cut it to a thousand manuscript pages and published it as one volume thick enough to serve as a makeshift high chair for Thanksgiving dinner.) But my books are mine, my work, with my name on them, and I edit them myself.

writing to a more exacting form, you may find it easier to proceed sequentially, making notes first, then drafting, then editing.

There are other kinds of editing besides the editing I've demonstrated writing this brief essay. Scientific and historical writing require much more careful attention to formal logic; fiction needs to be reviewed for fidelity to voice and point of view. Nor is editing ever really finished. Every sentence might be further improved, although it's also true that work can be overedited. The problem arises most acutely in the sentences embodying figures of speech, the very sentences on which I worked hardest in the drafting process you just followed with me. You can crank metaphors up only so tight before they begin to sound forced. The best editors I've worked with had what seemed to me an uncanny ability to single out for revision precisely those sentences I'd worked hardest to perfect. My editors may not have been psychic; they may simply have been alert to purple prose. James Dickey once wrote that he needed about one hundred fifty drafts of a poem to get it right and fifty more to make it sound spontaneous.

As you may have noticed following my editing example, you reach a point in editing where the words lie dead on the page, no longer evoking much emotional response as you reread them. Sometimes, proofreading a set of book galleys, I've found myself reading along thinking of something else entirely, my daydream strewing uncaught typos in its wake. When writing goes dead you need to put it away for a while. If you're writing against a deadline, you simply have to shake your head to clear away the cobwebs and focus your attention more closely on the words you've allowed familiarity to blur.

Because it's possible for those helpful strangers called editors to rework a piece of writing, people think of editing as somehow detachable—a separate, rational, Apollonian procedure worked upon the irrational, Dionysian creative draft. Editing is in fact simply *more writ-*

find your way to publication. It's even harder to make a living writing, and few writers do. Gertrude Stein had a theory about writing for a living, obviously derived from personal experience (although Stein had the advantage of inherited personal wealth):

> There is no doubt about it, in the twentieth century if you are to come to be writing really writing you cannot make a living at it no not by writing. It was done in the nineteenth century but not in the eighteenth or in the twentieth no not possibly. And that is very curious, not so curious really but still very curious. In the eighteenth century not enough read to make any one earn their living and in the twentieth century too many read for any one to make their living by writing, the nineteenth century was just right it was in between. Too few is as many as too many. The end of the nineteenth century already they could not make a living writing.[1]

Only a few thousand Americans make a living writing independently full time. I do, and have since 1970, when *Harper's* appointed me a contributing editor and I left employment at Hallmark Cards. For the next two decades I averaged about $25,000 a year (in today's dollars). These days I earn about as much annually from writing as a physician earns in general practice. A few people—we all know who they are—make a very good living writing, with incomes in the millions of dollars. But they're rare as rock stars. There probably aren't one hundred such writers in the world.

In 1980, two sociologists, Paul William Kingston and Jonathan R. Cole, conducted a survey of 2,241 authors for the Authors' Guild Foundation and the Columbia University Center for the Social Sciences. Among their sample they found median 1979 earnings from writing of $4,775:

Eight

BUSINESS

Most writers I've known take writing as a personal commitment first and last. Their need to write is deeply driven. Writing is important to them, and they would write whether they published or not. Their friends admire their dedication even if it sometimes seems quixotic; more skeptical observers suspect rampant egomania. (Sometimes egomania is a job requirement. I asked a neurosurgeon once why so many of his brethren seemed to be egomaniacs. He didn't miss a beat. "We have to be," he shot back. "We lose ninety-five percent of our patients.") An editor of my acquaintance who's seen too many manuscripts cross his desk in the course of a long and exhausting career told me I shouldn't write this book. "People don't need to be encouraged to write," he sneered. "They need to be *discouraged.* There's too much drivel out there already." I wouldn't want to be an unknown writer offering my first work to that man. Fortunately, he no longer edits beginning writers, so he can afford to indulge his cynicism.

Whatever its psychic origins, tenacity, not to say obstinance—the cluster of qualities that James Joyce called "silence, exile and cunning"—is a valuable asset if you want to write, because it's not easy to

> In short, half of American authors actually earned less than \$5,000 from their writing in that year. A quarter of all writers earned \$1,000 or less, and a tenth reported no income at all from writing in that year. The top 10 percent of writing income exceeded \$45,000 in 1979; the writing income of the top 5 percent exceeded \$80,000. But these were the rarified few. The central message of this study appeared almost at the outset: most authors cannot begin to make ends meet from their writing alone.[2]

Kingston and Cole estimate the median hourly return from writing among their sample at \$4.90 per hour. And notice also: the top 10 percent of writers surveyed averaged only about \$40 per hour. "If this figure represented the top of the profession," the sociologists comment, "it is one that still pales in comparison to the \$200 or more that top lawyers at major law firms billed per hour."[3] Double all these numbers to adjust for the decline in the value of the dollar since 1979, and they're still not extravagant.

Evidently, writing in America makes a better hobby than profession. Writers are so poorly compensated for their work that in genteel literary circles, among poets in particular, talk of compensation is considered socially offensive. The economist John Kenneth Galbraith once brilliantly observed that occupations are rewarded in America in inverse proportion to their perceived virtue. Thus movie stars are paid royally, teachers modestly, and mothers—because motherhood by general agreement is the noblest of attainments—not at all. On this principle, the literary intelligentsia judge writing at the median-income level (which is often their own writing) to be indubitably virtuous; poets, who make the least income for their labor-intensive work, they consider saints; while best-selling novelists prove out to be mere vulgarians.

It's true that writing for a living and what Gertrude Stein calls "really writing" can conflict, but the conflict is usually one of time, not of standards. I would certainly have written more of what I wanted to write and less of what editors assigned me if I'd had some other source of income, but I didn't. "Most authors must be subsidized," Cole and Kingston note; "other jobs and spouses are the modern-day patrons of our literature."[4] The detective fiction of Georges Simenon and Graham Greene subsidized their novels; who would begrudge them that subsidy given the results? Most "serious" novelists couldn't write a deliberately "commercial" novel if they tried (many have and failed), because commercial novels aren't merely inferior "literary" novels; they're a different form, written to different requirements. (Northrop Frye categorizes them as "highly conventionalized literature," a category that also includes naive and primitive writing.)[5] Nor, generally, can commercial novelists produce high art—it's a different form as well, one they haven't learned to write. If anyone thinks he can write like Sidney Sheldon, Sheldon's literary agent, Morton L. Janklow, likes to say, let him try it and see how he fares.

These are old and stale debates. Once you clear away the snobbery, high, medium, and low art turn out to be defined by their social histories as much as by any inherent qualities of art (any form can be artful within its terms—consider what Picasso did with the comic-book form in *Dream and Lie of Franco,* or Jonathan Swift with the travel narrative). Poetry was once high art (meaning what the gentry read), the novel trash. Now poetry is rarified almost out of existence, the novel is high art, and television is trash. Television will come to be used as an art form in its turn, at about the same time that some other popular medium replaces it that parents can warn their children against.

The truth is, most writers write as well as they can about what preoccupies them. Writers who do well commercially usually succeed because their preoccupations happen to match those of a wider audience of readers. Where literary writers are concerned, the wider audience is often what publishers call a "crossover" audience, meaning a set of readers interested in a particular subject who cross over to join readers loyal to a particular writer. My friend Tracy Kidder is a writer with a gift for celebrating ordinary experience and would certainly have come to a large audience sooner or later, but his first best-seller, *The Soul of a New Machine,* about a small company building a commercial computer, happened to appeal to a large crossover readership of businesspeople. Truman Capote found a large audience with *In Cold Blood* because the book attracted a major crossover of true-crime buffs. I conclude that subject matter has at least as much to do with commercial success as happy endings.

If your work doesn't require commercial publication, avoid it. The resulting serenity will add years to your life. George Berkemeier might have found an academic press willing to publish his biography of Andrew Drumm but sensibly decided instead to publish the book himself through a local printer. He earned back his costs selling copies to local-history buffs, friends, and Drumm alumni. Since the commercial market for poetry is small in the United States, many poets self-publish and offer their books at public readings. Genealogists can self-publish their family trees for relatives and descendants.

Desktop publishing opens up exciting new possibilities for writers. Edward Behr publishes a quarterly newsletter about food, *The Art of Eating,* from his home in Peacham, Vermont. Each twelve-page issue is devoted to one or two subjects ("California Sauvignon Blanc," "Potatoes," "The Atlantic Salmon," "Walnuts," "Honey Makers," "Farm-Raised Game Birds"), which Behr researches thoroughly and writes about with eloquent authority. A one-inch advertisement Behr placed in *The New Yorker* caught my wife's attention. Behr charges about as much as a national magazine charges for an annual subscription; for the knowledge he offers and the pleasure of reading his writing, we consider his self-published newsletter a bargain.

Other writers have self-published a book, set up a system for ordering by phone with a credit card or even by mail by check, advertised in periodicals such as *The New York Times Book Review,* and sold their book directly. The Yale graphic designer Edward Tufte has marketed two books this way, in best-selling quantities. The disadvantage of self-publishing is that you have to bear the risk and the expense yourself and develop a market (Tufte mortgaged his house); the advantage is that you receive all the return after costs. The approach works best for how-to books; I doubt if many self-published novels break even.

"Publish" originally meant to make something public; in that older sense of the word there are many ways to publish your writing besides commercially. You might incorporate it into letters. You might circulate it in manuscript to friends. You might read it aloud to guests after dinner. (I've done all these things.) You might offer it as required or extra work in school. You might contribute it to public forums such as newspaper and magazine letter-to-the-editor and op-ed pages. You might submit it to your alumni publication or to trade or technical journals. There are neighborhood newspapers looking for competent volunteer book reviewers and restaurant critics; all sorts of ephemeral publications such as church and other organizational bulletins have space to fill; and you can always start a newsletter or a 'zine of your own. (A 'zine is a homemade magazine people produce for fun.) I'm planning to self-publish my next work of fiction in the form of a 'zine, to take advantage of the formal and compositional possibilities of desktop publishing. I'll circulate my 'zine by subscription (or free, if no one wants to subscribe), while I continue writing verity under contract.

Electronic publishing is a new and promising opportunity. *Rolling Stone* media critic Jon Katz described it in a recent article:

> Our creative lives have changed. As happened when the printing press, the telephone and television were invented, stories and the means by which we tell them will never be the same, not for the people who tell them or for those who take them in. All over the world, the gatekeepers are disintegrating as the few who always decided what stories the rest of us would hear are yielding to the millions telling their stories directly to one another. . . . Every day, those who can afford the computer equipment and the telephone bills can be their own producers, agents, editors and audiences. . . . The roads on which these stories move are the computer bulletin board systems. There are more than 33,000 of them in the United States and more than 11 million Americans are using them.[6]

On computer bulletin boards, people tell each other real-life stories. They joke, commiserate, and philosophize—sharing, says Katz, "the communal experiences of life, death, work, love, family." One advantage of the new medium is that it's informal. "The tellers are preoccupied with the stories themselves, not the manner in which they are presented."[7]

These and many other media offer you a place to publish or to practice. You aren't confined to commercial channels. There are tens of thousands of publishing opportunities open in the United States if you're willing to accept little or no compensation for your work. For many people, including people who are just beginning to write, compensation is secondary to the validating experience of appearing in print.

In any case, print is the final step, not the first. People who have never published anything sometimes ask me if they should send a query letter to a magazine or a publisher before undertaking a work of writing. I suggest they might want to do some writing first, and they look at me anxiously and fade away. I always wonder what planet they live on. Why should a businessperson—and editors are businesspeople, not patrons or creative writing teachers—take a chance without evidence on an unknown writer? If it were your money, would you?

If I haven't discouraged you from the preposterous notion of breaking into print,* let's talk about the business of writing. That's what writers talk about when they get together, not aesthetics or ideas. Intellectuals talk about aesthetics and ideas. Writers grouse about their publishers. "All your friends say the same thing," Ginger nudges me. "They say when they went on national tour or Oprah or whatever, there weren't any books in the stores." It's true. Heartbreaking but true. Publishers arrange it that way to torture us.

Most writers of verity start out writing shorter forms. They're newspaper reporters, book reviewers, magazine writers. Some of them then make the transition to books. They have credibility because they have a file of articles or reviews they've written that they can show and they often have a subject on which their short-form work has made them an authority. David Halberstam was chairman of the Harvard *Crimson* and a small-town-newspaper reporter before he began reporting from Vietnam. John McPhee accumulated fifteen years of *New Yorker* rejections before the magazine began buying his work. Joan Didion wrote about her native state, California, for magazines. Tom Wolfe wrote for a Sunday newspaper supplement after earning a Ph.D. in American Studies at Yale. Book editors watch out for such people and recruit them (as I was recruited) if they don't come knocking on their own.

* I'm kidding, of course.

Fiction writers may also start out writing shorter forms. Some accumulate a credible collection in much the same way verity writers accumulate a file. Larry Brown, a fireman in Mississippi, broke into print that way:

> I figured writing might be like learning how to build houses or lay brick, or even fight fires. I had one burning thought that I believed was true. If I wrote long enough and hard enough, I'd eventually learn how. My only obligation was feeding my family while I was trying to learn how to do this other thing, and that meant to keep working at the fire department plus the usual extra stuff like carrying bricks and mixing mortar and swinging a hammer and cutting pulpwood with a chain saw. But I was willing to do all that in order to have the scattered afternoons and weekends to write. From 1980 on I wrote steadily, filling up pages, mailing off manuscripts, publishing a story every couple of years and then finally a first book of stories in 1988. There've been two novels and another book of stories since then.[8]

There are far fewer outlets for short fiction in the United States than for short verity. Of several approaches to finding a publisher for fiction, my impression is that two predominate. One is participating in a creative writing program and networking through teachers and alumni, which is self-explanatory. The other is networking ad hoc. Both these approaches apply to verity as well, except that most writing programs outside of journalism schools exclude verity from their curriculum or give it short shrift (this particular snobbery is abating, however).

Networking ad hoc means, essentially, finding the right strings and pulling them. The strings you need to find are those that lead to an agent and/or a publisher: a writer, an editor, an agent, a publishing salesperson, or anyone who works for, is related to, or knows any of these personages. You may meet these people at writers' conferences, library and bookstore appearances, or other public events. When you do, you will have to overcome the proverbial shyness that afflicts fledgling writers and attempt to convince them to look over your work and either consider sponsoring it themselves or passing it along with an endorsement to someone who can. The person who is most likely to do you this favor is someone who has interests similar to those manifested in your work. If you write about intimate family relationships, don't ask an orphan to sponsor your book. If you celebrate war, don't expect help from a pacifist.

It isn't fair that you should have the burden not only of writing but also of politicking shamelessly to find support for your work. You ought to be able to write a query letter and receive a prompt and courteous reply.* Unfortunately, the world doesn't work that way. Very few people ever acquire jobs by sending around résumés; people get jobs by knowing someone, by sticking a foot in the door, by cornering someone and selling themselves, by hook or by crook. Publishing works the same way, for the same reason: there are too many people chasing too few slots. Rather than favoritism, you might think of the networking business I'm describing as a rough-and-ready first sort. I don't buy products from strangers who turn up at my door, and publishers don't buy books from over-the-transom slush piles. I used to remind my children, when they complained about having to read the directions, that the universe is an IQ test. If you can't figure out how to get past the front door, why should anyone believe you're clever enough to write a book?

* * *

* In fact, if you have a finished manuscript you want an editor to look at and can identify a particular editor who might be interested, *do* write a query letter; it will at least get you past the slush pile. But don't stop there.

Until you have something to sell, you don't need an agent. You may not need an agent even then. When Richard Kluger called me from Atheneum to propose that I write a book about the Middle West, I was in no position to argue about the terms of my contract, so I didn't seek out an agent. I took what Atheneum offered, which was the standard deal of the day, a hardcover royalty of 10 percent of the retail selling price on the first 5,000 copies, 12.5 percent on the next 2,500 copies and 15 percent thereafter, and a 50-50 split of any book club and paperback earnings.

I did acquire an agent before I negotiated my second book. By then I was a contributing editor at *Harper's* (which simply meant they listed my name on the masthead and promised to look at the articles I sent them) and I'd published a book to good reviews, which had sold a few thousand copies and had been listed as one of the hundred best books of the year by the *New York Times*. So I had a modest reputation to offer that presumably translated, commercially speaking, into a set of devoted readers numbering somewhat greater than zero. I found an agent by asking Kluger to give me the names of three agents who he felt were the best he'd worked with. I traveled to New York at my own expense and interviewed the three agents, all men. The first was too literary. He made a point of showing me the bottle of whiskey he kept in his desk à la Hemingway, which even in my drinking days I considered frivolous. The second was too austere. The third, a former book editor named John Cushman, an avuncular Harvard man, now sadly deceased, told me gruffly that his job wasn't literary, his job was selling books. We shook hands on the spot.

Agents make good partners, particularly if you don't live in New York (but even if you do). If they're competent they know the going rates and the best terms; they know which editors might be interested in your work. Don't ask them for literary judgments about your projects. They'll give them and you'll be sorry you asked. (My agent friends will kill me for saying so, but literary acumen ain't their forte.

Nor should it be—that's your job.) They'll cost you at least ten, more usually fifteen percent of your writing income. You should see evidence as you go along that their contribution of contacts and negotiating expertise adds at least that much to the total (and if it doesn't add more, you ought to look elsewhere). They can increase your return by successfully boosting your asking price or by negotiating better terms. A 55-45 paperback split in your favor is a valuable improvement over a 50-50 split if your book wins a major reprint sale; 15 percent on every hardcover copy sold is better than a standard 10–12.5–15 percent scale.

Agents serve other useful purposes besides selling articles and books. Publishers sometimes approach agents with projects, which they then throw your way. They negotiate contracts (some these days are lawyers). They track, collect, and disburse payments and can bring leverage to bear if a payment is behind. *Esquire* once refused to pay my expenses for an article it commissioned from me that it subsequently rejected; the agent who arranged my participation finally extracted a check by threatening to block the magazine's access to another client far more prestigious than I. Agents can serve as bad cops to your good cop in your relations with editors and publishers, sparing you pain. They have up-to-date experience with markets and trends. Some are affiliated with Hollywood agents and serve as a pipeline for writing projects with screenplay potential. Through my New York agent, Janklow & Nesbit Associates, and their affiliate Creative Artists Associates, my memoir, *A Hole in the World,* was optioned for film; eventually I wrote the screenplay under contract to New Regency Productions. Besides market intelligence and business services, agents can offer support and friendship in what is sometimes a lonely profession. Mine have and do, and I cherish them.

Literary Market Place, published annually by R. R. Bowker, lists literary agents, but a bare list won't do you much good. You'll have to network to track down the agent who's right for you. I strongly recommend you interview agents in person; the agent-author relationship is a marriage of sorts.

A brief Book Note reported by Sarah Lyall in the *New York Times* demonstrates how valuable, not to say saintly, an agent can be:

> If you're an author, it helps to have a high tolerance for rejection. Consider Daniel Evan Weiss. His first novel, *The Roaches Have No King*, about a group of hip, philosophizing New York cockroaches keenly interested in the love life of the man in whose apartment they live, was turned down by more than two dozen publishers when he began sending it around six years ago. . . .
>
> But he didn't give up, and neither did his agent, Joy Harris, who found publishers for the book in England . . . and in Germany. And finally, she found a publisher here in the United States, thirteen years after Mr. Weiss, now 40, began working on the book. Several weeks ago, *The Roaches Have No King* was published by High Risk Books, the new American imprint of Serpent's Tail Press, a British company. . . . [The publisher] said that the company had sold out its first printing of 5,000 books—not bad at all for a first novel at a small imprint—and had gone back for a second printing of 5,000 more.
>
> Mr. Weiss, who has written several other novels and nonfiction books . . . said that before High Risk came along, the rejections had so numbed him that he had almost given up altogether. Now, he says, he'll no longer have to buy copies of the British version and give them out as gifts. . . .[9]

Notice that the return on Ms. Harris's expenditure of time across the years was around $2,000 (15 percent of 15 percent of 5,000 copies at, say, $20 per copy) plus whatever small sums the British and German editions earned. Bless her. Notice also that the author grossed around $15,000 on 5,000 copies, less his agent's $2,000 = $13,000, out of which he had to reserve income tax and, if he was writing full time, self-employment Social Security. Not a bountiful return on a year or more of work writing the novel and thirteen years biting his nails. Writers joke that they earn a nickel an hour. Kingston and Cole would say $4.90 or so. Knowing the extent to which writing fills a writer's every waking moment (and, often, her sleeping moments as well), I'd bet on the nickel. So the literary intelligentsia are right—"really writing" is untainted by commerce after all.

Now. Publishers. A subject about which every writer I know can generate a jeremiad or two—of picayune advances, bad copyediting, poor design, pitiful prepublication sales, and tardy and inadequate distribution. All these complaints settle down around the same issue, which is how much support a publisher gives a book (and its author).

Unfortunately, that support isn't routinely written into book contracts. A publisher legally obligates himself to do not much more than typeset, print, and bind a book; all the rest is judgment and negotiation. With rare exceptions, book contracts don't specify either advertising or promotion budgets. It would be nice if they did, but the combined efforts of authors, agents, and the Authors Guild haven't been able to make that happen yet. Nor, in my experience, do publishing staffs want authors poking around the publishing house, telling them their business. It's your editor's job to cheerlead your book through the house. The trouble is, yours isn't the only book he has to convince the editorial, promotion, sales, and advertising departments to support. You can help with ideas, angles, suggestions of potential markets your publisher may not have considered. But you'll find yourself oddly outside the packaging process. I call myself the pot roast. That's how it feels to be discussed, organized, packaged, and shipped without being consulted. Writers scream at their publishers a lot. Publishing staffs, distracted by organizational duties, have largely gone deaf under the assault.

At the same time, it's clear that authors can boost their books if they're willing to spend their time boosting rather than, say, going on to writing their next book. Jacqueline Susann famously used to turn up at dawn at her publisher's loading docks to flirt with the truck-drivers delivering her best-selling novels across America, to speed them on their way. She was an indefatigable visitor of bookstores in every city where she traveled; besides charming the booksellers, she always moved her latest book to prominent display in the front of the store. Every published writer has to decide how much time and energy he's willing to devote to promotion. Sometimes publishing a book can feel like running for President, with campaign stops and babies to kiss in city after city until the skylines blur. Thomas Pynchon has the right idea; he's the man who wasn't there. If we all ducked and covered, though, the Celebrities would swarm in to fill the empty ecological niche we left. They do anyway, like cowbirds pushing little songbirds out of their nests. There was a time not long ago when the top three books on the *New York Times* hardcover nonfiction best-seller list were all nonbooks by nonwriters: Rush Limbaugh, Jerry Seinfeld, and Howard Stern. I'll refrain from predicting the decline of the Republic; the truth is, most Americans don't read real books.

Wisely or unwisely, I let my editors develop my books in-house. I send them ideas along the way and make myself available for any promotional work that looks to justify the investment of time. Contacts with booksellers sell books, especially prepublication. I did dozens of radio interviews after *The Making of the Atomic Bomb* was published, some of them lasting several hours. I never saw any obvious increase in sales in the areas the stations reached, so I've stopped doing radio except for a few select programs that reach nationwide. I do television and print interviews. Lectures and readings sell books. Book tours sell books—I can tell, because people line up and I sign copies and hear the cash register ring.

Publishers will identify me from this discussion as a mid-list author, profitable but not best-selling. Publishing is a business, and authors who bring in millions of dollars earn corresponding support. When I set out in 1986 to write about a Missouri farm family, the story that became my book *Farm,* a rural banker charged me humorously to find out the answer to the ultimate rural question: Did the (quality of the) land make the farmer or the farmer (by his work of improvement) make the land? Publishing has its chicken-or-egg counterpart: Which comes first, the publisher's support of the book or the book's support of the publisher? After watching Jack Nicholson, in the movie *Wolf,* drive all the way to Vermont to sign up a writer, my friends and I tried to decide what Vermont writer would justify such attention. We concluded it had to be either Aleksandr Solzhenitsyn or God. Either one would command a large advance—for the right project.

Fortunately, first books sometimes receive special attention. An ambitious young editor may want to prove herself while developing her own "stable" of writers (as we're revealingly grouped). For a writer starting out, that's a nice windfall.

It's easy to believe that publishers are doing you a favor publishing your book, a sanctification of their function they're in no hurry to correct. Take another look at the Daniel Evan Weiss story if you believe publishing houses are eleemosynary institutions. Those five thousand copies that brought Weiss perhaps $15,000 in royalties netted his publisher $45,000. That amount more than covers the cost of printing, binding, and shipping five thousand copies plus the time it took the publicity person to call the *New York Times* to report the good deed. It's a good rule of thumb that publishers make a profit long before an author earns back her advance.

A writer's best attitude toward a publisher, I think, is one of alert pragmatism. Publishing is a business, and publishers are business people. They don't overvalue either charitable good works or literary excellence, nor should they be expected to. Like you, they want to sell your book. Unlike you, they have other books to sell as well. It follows that they have exactly as much right to your loyalty as their performance justifies.

Magazine writing is altogether more straightforward than book publishing. You can find an editor's name on the masthead of a magazine, send him your bona fides and a brief proposal, and expect a response. If it's a good idea and he likes your stuff, you may have an assignment even if you're an unknown. You normally sell only first-serial rights—the right to publish the story first in magazine form before its publication elsewhere—so that any further use, such as inclusion in an anthology, can bring you further return. The magazine pays your travel and research expenses. You can usually negotiate a kill fee of up to fifty percent of your payment as compensation for your time if the magazine rejects ("kills") the article you submit.

Magazine payments vary across a wide range, from less than $1,000 for an article of average length, 3,000–5,000 words, to (rarely) $20,000 or more. Few magazines pay more than a dollar a word, a payment base that hasn't changed much over the years, probably because there's always a pool of talented, eager younger writers willing to work for less than established writers can afford. (A magazine article seldom takes less than a month of hard work, often two or three.) I hate to encourage such scabbing, but it represents a valuable opportunity to writers trying to break out from local and regional publication. Magazine writing is the one kind of journalism I know that benefits directly from corporate writing experience. Don Erickson, the managing editor of *Esquire* during the 1960s, its hottest years, was appointed to that position directly from the editorship of a glossy corporate house organ. I was still writing for Hallmark house organs when *Esquire* published "Death All Day in Kansas." James Morgan, who trained under me at Hallmark, went on to edit *TWA Ambassador* before becoming articles editor at *Playboy,* after which he returned to his native Arkansas to write articles and books on his own. Mark Singer went directly from the *Yale Alumni Magazine* to *The New Yorker.*

Writing for one magazine can lead to writing for others. You can send along a proposal and a tear sheet, or another magazine may give you a call. I heard from *Playboy* out of the blue one day in 1972 after publishing for two years almost exclusively in *Harper's.* That was the quarter-horse-racing assignment. After that *Playboy* proposed I move my family to Florida for three months at the magazine's expense to write about the destruction of the Everglades. My wife and two small children enjoyed a gourmet month at a house on the beach in Naples, while I slogged through the Big Cypress swamp slathered with mosquito repellent, looking for alligator nests. Other assignments followed. Other magazines called. I called other magazines. I learned to write to length, an odd talent that arrived unbidden: if I was asked to deliver 3,000 or 5,000 words, the article emerged at the appropriate length on first draft (remember that I was scrambling to support myself with magazine writing; desperation set the alarm on my word clock and shaped the article en passant).

I learned a basic truth of magazine writing in those busy years: if it's the editor's idea, whatever you turn in is already ninety percent sold. Writing on assignment demanded flexibility. I bring up my bibliography of magazine articles and find the following:

"Ike: An Artist in Iron." *Harper's,* July 1970. Abr. *Reader's Digest,* Sept. 1970. (A reassessment of the character of Dwight D. Eisenhower.) . . .

"The Boy Who Didn't Die." *Redbook,* Aug. 1971. Abr.

Reader's Digest, Dec. 1971. (Profile of the only known human rabies survivor.) . . .

"The Geritol Days of Lawrence Welk." *Audience,* Mar.–Apr. 1972. (A visit with the champagne-music man.) . . .

" 'Deep Throat' Goes Down in Memphis." *Playboy,* Oct. 1976. (Pornography on trial.) . . .

"The Plundered Province Revisited." *American Heritage,* Sept. 1978. (Strip-mining the West.) . . .

"God Pity a One-Dream Man." *American Heritage,* 1980. (The life of rocket pioneer Robert Goddard.) . . .

"Home to the Ozarks." *Reader's Digest,* Nov. 1981. (Familiar trails.) . . .

"You Can Control Your Dreams." *Parade,* Feb. 19, 1984. (The discovery of lucid dreaming.) . . .

"A Yield Against the Odds." *Harper's,* Apr. 1987. (Harvest time on a Missouri farm.)

I did reports as well on nuclear power, rape, biology, Gerald Ford, the 1976 Republican National Convention, the early days of the cocaine craze, California, an old skywriter, thermonuclear fusion, the breaching of the Berlin Wall, the last wild horses, energy independence, telescopes, senility, extended orgasm, suburban values, you name it. I also ghostwrote two books and edited two more. In the interstices of this mad scrambling, I wrote and saw published four novels and eight works of verity all my own.

Magazine writing requires a high tolerance for financial anxiety. No one ever got rich writing for magazines. It's a decent living, but it's contract labor, one time through, not entrepreneurship. When you undertake to write a book you assume greater risk, psychic as well as financial, but you also chance greater reward. Working for a corporation rescued me from unemployment following military demobilization; magazine writing rescued me from the anonymity of the corporation. Magazine writing gave my book projects credibility to publishers at a far higher level than any number of proposals and endorsements might have done. I worked at it for years before I realized I was living out a childhood dream. Richard Halliburton's *Book of Marvels* and *Second Book of Marvels*, episodic narratives of adventures visiting exotic places around the world, had been my favorite books when I was a child. Unconsciously, writing for magazines, I had devised a way to accumulate adventures of my own. I never had myself commissioned as a boat so that I could swim the Panama Canal, but Halliburton never visited the Kurchatov Institute in Moscow and touched the external graphite shell of the first nuclear reactor outside North America.

Foundation grants can be a significant source of funds for writing. They're a source that many writers remain unaware of or overlook. I've had nine foundation grants since 1972, all but one of them for writing. The least amount I've been granted for a single project was $12,000, the most $100,000. I undertook to write *The Making of the Atomic Bomb* without grant support, but the research and writing would have been unendurably prolonged if grants had not been forthcoming along the way.

Most of the largest foundations in the United States are centered in New York, but every large city has local foundations, often clustered together under a common umbrella, that give grants to projects they consider worthy. The first grant I received came from the Kansas City Association of Trusts and Foundations, not long after I left Hallmark Cards, when I was struggling to establish myself as an independent journalist. I knew the director of the association because I had worked with him on a committee organized to save Kansas City's decaying city hospitals. I went to him in some desperation and simply told him my problem. One of the organizations his association funded was a consortium of local and regional small colleges; he thought a writer who was publishing in national magazines could bring valuable information to students at the consortium's schools. In exchange for devoting part of each week through the school year speaking to classes at seven different colleges in turn, I got a sum sufficient to put me on my feet, something like half a year's income. It was a godsend; I was dead broke.

What could you do that might be of value to local foundations? That would depend on their particular interests. You might talk or give readings at schools, colleges, hospitals, retirement homes, or prisons. You might develop a pilot writing program for such institutions. You might undertake to write a history of the area or even of the foundation itself.

Foundations are like banks. They don't simply give money away; they invest to develop their real or abstract communities, fully expecting a return. Like banks, they're required to determine your creditworthiness, except that the assets they value are cultural rather than financial. As with banks also, the first "loan"—the first grant—is the hardest one to get, because that's presumably when you have the least cultural collateral. That's why I suggest you look into local foundations before approaching the big nationals. One grant leads to another, because a grant received and successfully fulfilled accredits you, certifying to another foundation that you're grantable. Grant officers, like bank officers, tend to know and trust each other and speak a common language in which to assess your grantworthiness.

I don't mean these statements cynically. I don't believe in "grantsmanship," whatever that is. If your credentials aren't in order or your work isn't up to standard, you won't qualify or won't continue to qualify for foundation support; foundation officers aren't fools. Writing is honorable work, and it's certainly not dishonest to assess realistically the sources of income available to support you while you pursue it.

One necessary component of grant applications is authoritative recommendations. I've always been shameless about asking notables of my acquaintance for recommendations. If you have confidence in yourself and your project, why not? Eventually a group of people around a table will look over your bona fides and decide whether or not they want to fund you; it's their privilege and their decision, not yours. They certainly won't give you a grant if you don't apply.

Grants normally can't be awarded directly to individuals. Tax regulations require foundations to offer grants in open competition through some form of collective review. For several years, for example, I was a member of an advisory committee to the Alfred P. Sloan Foundation, a large New York foundation established by one of the founders of General Motors to educate the public about science and technology. Sloan officers assembled this particular committee to advise on grant selection for books on the history of twentieth-century technology to be written with foundation support. Each writer whose project the foundation commissioned would receive a $100,000 grant plus a $25,000 expense budget.

Not wanting to inundate themselves with grant proposals, Sloan officers alerted the professional writing community to the program by word of mouth (which demonstrates the importance of networking). Officers and advisers called writers they knew who specialized in writing about technology. In one case, I called a young writer whose outstanding first book I had just read as a judge for the National Book Award and convinced him to apply (he won a grant to write about the commercialization of space). To add prestige to the series we courted writers of the stature of David McCullough—unsuccessfully, in his case. Applicants submitted detailed proposals for histories of radar, television, the digital computer, the laser, modern agriculture, biotechnology, commercial aviation, noninvasive bio-imaging, and similar topics, most of which, predictably, had never been written about at full scale. In the end we commissioned some twenty books. We rejected another ten or fifteen proposals because they didn't meet our particular criteria.

There's an exception to the rule of open competition for grants: foundation officers are allowed to award what are called "officer grants" of up to a certain amount—in 1994 it was $30,000—without peer review. They can be lifesaving. When I undertook to write the book that became *The Making of the Atomic Bomb,* I prepared a thorough seventy-five-page proposal that included a draft chapter. Michael Korda at Simon & Schuster liked the proposal—he told me later it was the best book proposal he'd ever seen—and offered a $75,000 advance. The advance was structured, as usual, in thirds: $25,000 on signing, $25,000 upon delivery of the first half of the manuscript, $25,000 upon delivery of the complete manuscript. Hidden in that customary structure is a gap that every independent writer abhors: the long, unfunded period up front when you're doing the research necessary before writing can begin. In my case, that research required three very full-time years. I had two children in high school, going into college; $25,000 wasn't going to meet my financial needs for the four years I would need to get to the halfway mark.

Magazine work just about pays its own way. If I had tried to make up the difference with magazine writing, that is, I would have been researching and writing for magazines full time and would have had no time to research the history of the atomic bomb. I made an occasional magazine assignment pay by proposing articles that in some way overlapped the subject of my book, but they delayed the book as much as they helped it.

One day an advertisement turned up in the *New York Review of Books* for a Ford Foundation program to commission books on significant aspects of international relations. I applied and won a grant—about a year's income, as I recall, plus a budget for travel. Farther down the road I ghostwrote a popular medical book for a Stanford psychiatrist that brought another half year's income for three months' work (and continues to pay royalties all these years later). With these various props supporting me, I finished three years' research and began writing *The Making of the Atomic Bomb.* I reached the halfway mark and collected the next segment of advance from Simon & Schuster. I kept going. Taxes came due. With her mother's help, my wife and I had managed to pay off the mortgage on our house. We took out a loan against our equity and I wrote on. That money ran out. My children were both attending college at the same time by then, and college bills piled up. I was still perhaps five hundred pages away from finishing but couldn't identify any source of funds that would allow me to continue. Nor could I simply tuck the manuscript away on a shelf; I'd accepted advances and a grant to write it, and it would soon be due.

I'd been in touch with the Sloan Foundation about some documents they happened to hold relating to atomic bomb history. Now in desperation I wrote to the officer with whom I'd corresponded, Arthur L. Singer, Jr., told him my dilemma, and enclosed several chapters of my book. He wrote back asking to see the rest of the book and mentioning the possibility of an officer grant. I delivered twenty more chapters to him the next day by Federal Express. After Art and his colleagues had reviewed them, he offered me $20,000, the maximum allowable at that time. I accepted gratefully. The Sloan grant rescued me. It kept my kids in college and enabled me to finish my book. When *The Making of the Atomic Bomb* won a Pulitzer Prize, Art told me he thought the foundation had made a good investment.

The National Endowment for the Arts, the National Endowment for the Humanities, the major national foundations, regional and community foundations, are all potential sources of funds for writing. They have income they're required by law to give away, every year. I recommend that you learn more about them.

* * *

Finally, there's Hollywood. Writing a screenplay must look easy, since everybody in America seems to have one in the works. It's not easy at all; it's comparable to constructing a cuckoo clock blindfolded. Writing a screenplay, Robert Towne once said, means writing a detailed description of a work of art. That's a little tony for my taste, but it catches the oddness of the form—it's like composing an elephantine, one-hundred-twenty-page haiku.

We're talking about business at this point, however, not craft. From a business perspective, the pay is good for screenplay writing, but the work is lousy. If you've been independent, work for hire is a shock. Anyone up the hierarchy, including a twenty-two-year-old snot fresh out of Princeton who happens to gofer your producer, is allowed to tell you how to fix your first or second or third or infinituple draft. "I know! Let's make the main character a serial killer!" "I know! Let's make the love interest a frog!" If you've invested any heart at all in your screenplay, you'll feel it breaking. I made it through three drafts of the screenplay of my memoir of childhood, *A Hole in the World.* The people I was working for were literate and reasonably civilized. But they wanted me to characterize as a loser the brother who saved my life as a child by going to the police to report that he and I were being brutally abused. He needed to fail, they thought, to balance my success. But he didn't fail, I insisted. Ah, well, they said, you can't just stick to the facts—this is fiction. Where had I heard *that* before? I told them I couldn't write my brother that way, whereupon we parted company.

Obviously I'm the wrong person to talk to about writing screenplays. Screenwriters have good benefits, always a danger signal—entrepreneurs don't get benefits. You have to join the screenwriters' guild. There's a hefty initiation fee, but the medical plan is fabulous. The guild has negotiated an excellent pay scale that depends not on the producer's approval but only on the physical delivery of the goods. Each draft, each "polish," has a definition and a fee, and the guild makes sure you collect.

Hemingway had the right idea about Hollywood. If they want to buy your book, he said, negotiate the price, load the manuscript into the back of the truck, and drive to the California-Nevada border at midnight. "Psst! Throw over the money!" When the bundle of money comes over, toss over your book and get the hell out. I feel good belonging to a union, but I wouldn't accept another screenplay commission on a bet.

Nine

OTHER VOICES

I've talked now through a pile of pages; I'd like to let a few other writers talk for a chapter, to widen the perspective. I hadn't planned to include a chapter like this one, but I got to reading Anthony Trollope's *Autobiography,* and the man made so much good sense that I decided I needed a sort of interchapter quoting him at length. I was going to call the interchapter "Mrs. Trollope's Boy," because Trollope's mother sustained her entire family by writing (most famously, *The Domestic Manners of the Americans*), and Anthony followed in her footsteps and did the same for his. ("She was at her [writing] table at four in the morning," Trollope says of his remarkable mother, "and had finished her work before the world had begun to be aroused."[1]) Then, in the course of my day-to-day reading, with the curious fortuity of preoccupation, I began noticing other discussions of writing that seemed valuable to add. I'm sure someone could multiply such useful passages to the length of an anthology, *Writers (and Others) on Writing.* (That's a good idea for a book—you can have it free of charge. Book ideas are easy to come by. It's making them into books and finding someone to publish them that's hard.)

The most laconic statement I found came from an interview with William T. Vollman, the best and most original new writer of his young generation. In his first seven years of publication, beginning in 1987, Vollman produced nine books of fiction and verity, all of them long, complicated, and ferociously original. To explain that phenomenal production, he told the *Washington Post*:

> Every place I go I have a notebook, and every time I see something interesting I make a point of stopping and writing it down. I put the notes into the computer and start working.

That's nearly as succinct as the Knickerbocker Rule.

Fran Lebowitz was interviewed in the Summer 1993 issue of the *Paris Review.* The interviews in George Plimpton's magazine are required reading for beginning writers, the inside skinny from the horses' mouths. The *Paris Review* has been interviewing writers at length, and publishing the edited results, for years, and the best interviews have been assembled into several book-length collections. I interviewed Kurt Vonnegut, Jr., for the review before Kurt became famous. Three other people interviewed him farther down the road; the editors eventually let Kurt assemble our various versions of him into one. He made the interviewer sound hostile and a little dense but kept all *his* best lines.

Lebowitz claims to hate to work. To explain one consequence of what she calls her profound slothfulness, she tells this story:

> LEBOWITZ: I was once at Sotheby's looking at some furniture. Just looking. This guy whom I knew came over and asked if I'd like to look at a Twain manuscript that was going to be for sale. I constantly have to disabuse people of the notion that I can afford things like Twain manuscripts. I said I'd love to look at it but I can't afford it. He showed it to me. A short story. He was telling me about the manuscript and where they found it and everything.

> He said, "I'm pretty knowledgeable about Twain, but there's one thing we don't understand. We've called in a Twain scholar."
>
> I said, "What is that?"
>
> He said, "See these little numbers? There are these little numbers every so often. We just don't know what those are."
>
> I said, "I do. I happen not to be a Twain scholar, but I happen to be a scholar of little numbers written all over the place. He was counting the words."
>
> The Sotheby's man said, "What are you talking about? That's ridiculous!"
>
> I said, "I bet you anything. Count."
>
> He counted the words and saw that I was right. He said, "Twain must've been paid by the word."
>
> I said, "It may have nothing to do with being paid by the word." Twain might have told himself he had to write this many words a day, and he would wonder, Am I there yet? Like a little kid in the back of a car: Are we there yet?[2]

The craftspeople who built the great medieval cathedrals probably counted the day's laying of stones.

E. L. Doctorow's 1994 novel, *The Waterworks,* set in Manhattan in the 1870s, is a rich, sinister tale. Random House published it at about the same time they published a selection of Doctorow's essays, *Jack London, Hemingway, and the Constitution.* Reviewing both books in the *New Republic,* Andrew Delbanco finds contrasts between them that demonstrate significant differences in craft:

> Many of Doctorow's points [in his essays] border on cant. He is not an essayist. The most arresting piece in this collection is

the least discursive. It is the one that was not commissioned—a brief rumination called "Standards," about the "self-referential power" of songs. A charming imaginative frolic, it moves among associated topics that include the origins of lullabies in mothers' crooning, the mixture of irony and militancy in wartime songs like "Goober Peas," the "compensatory" function of ballads about lost love. But when, in the other essays, he turns away from the associative mode and becomes resolutely expository in the service of an argument, he tends to sound callow and even pontifical. Here is a piece written before the 1992 election out of disgust at George Bush and with high hopes for Bill Clinton:

> The true president would have the strength to widen the range of current political discourse, and would love and revere language as the best means we have to close on reality. That implies a sensibility attuned to the immense moral consequence of every human life. Perhaps even a sense of tragedy that would not let him sleep the night through.

Weakened by this mixture of outrage and sentimentality, the essays are more an expression of an offended sensibility than a serious effort at political analysis or understanding. They have a thin, sloganeering quality—and, finally, a columnist's transience. But when, in *The Waterworks,* the same sentiments are realized as images and put to use within the context of a story of loss and rescue, they work to greater effect. "I have dreamt sometimes," says [Doctorow's contemporary narrator, who writes with elisions],

> . . . that if it were possible to lift this littered, paved Manhattan from the earth . . . and all its torn and dripping

> pipes and conduits and tunnels and tracks and cables—all of it, like a scab from new skin underneath—how seedlings would sprout, and freshets bubble up, and brush and grasses would grow over the rolling hills. . . . A season or two of this and the mute, protesting culture buried for so many industrial years under the tenements and factories . . . would rise again . . . of the lean, religious Indians of the bounteous earth. . . . Such love I have for those savage polytheists of my mind . . . such envy for the inadequate stories they told each other, their taxonomies, cosmologies . . . their lovely dreams of the world they stood on and who was holding it up. . . .[3]

For another writer—probably for Delbanco, the reviewer—the balance might have tipped the other way. Good novelists are rarely intellectuals; intellectuals are rarely good novelists. Iris Murdoch, the novelist and Oxford philosopher, is both, but in *Metaphysics as a Guide to Morals* she gives priority to the creators:

> It may be that the best model for all thought is the creative imagination. . . . Novelists . . . have constantly to invent methods of conveying states of mind or to choose between different styles of doing so. Novels moreover exhibit the ubiquity of moral quality inherent in consciousness. We may rightly criticize novels in which characters' thoughts (as well as actions) exhibit a lack of moral sensibility which seems called for by the story. This is an important kind of literary criticism. Indeed the judgment passed upon the moral sensibility of the artist is a primary kind of esthetic judgment. Of course, some artists can talk about how they work and others cannot, or will not, and it is the art object which is great or otherwise, and not the "how it is done." Artists are famous for not knowing how it is done, or

> for perhaps rightly feeling that at their best they do not know what they are up to. . . . At any rate, the novelist's problem (the traditional novelist's problem), solved intuitively or otherwise, is precisely a unification of fact and value, the exhibiting of personal morality in a non-abstract manner as the stuff of consciousness.[4]

"A unification of fact and value" is an excellent definition, it seems to me, of any given word in any given language. So words bloom into novels (or verities), and the large problem grows out of the small: to assemble words so they work together with something approaching the same force of unified fact and value that each word has accrued in its long, accumulating passage through history. Words are the model, words are the tools, words are the boards, words are the nails.

Structures of meaning larger and more diffuse than words also loom up and have to be confronted when you prepare to write. The last thing I know, when I finish writing a book, is why I really wrote it. Then I see that it elaborates on something personal, usually something from childhood. John McPhee, talking to Norman Sims in *The Literary Journalists*, makes the same discovery:

> "There really are lots of ideas going by," McPhee said. "A huge stream of ideas. What makes somebody choose one over another? If you make a list of all the work I've ever done, and put a little mark beside things that relate to activities and interests I had before I was twenty, you'd have a little mark beside well over 90 percent of the pieces of writing. That is no accident.
>
> "Paul Fussell said he wrote about the First World War as a way of expressing himself about his own experiences in the Second World War. That makes *complete* sense. Why did I write

about tennis players? Why did I write about a basketball player? Why hold this person up for scrutiny and not that one? Because you've got some personal interest that relates to your own life. It's an important theme about anybody's writing."[5]

Sharon O'Brien's *Willa Cather: The Emerging Voice* is a biography of the American novelist up to the time *O Pioneers!* was published and her public career began; researching and writing the biography demanded from O'Brien more than one kind of emergence herself:

> At first, I didn't think I was writing a biography; instead, I saw myself embarking on a consideration of Cather's life and work from a feminist perspective. I was intrigued by her transition from a young journalist who praised masculine values and scorned female pastimes to a mature writer who firmly united womanhood and creativity. I sensed that this development had helped her to find her voice as a writer. Willa Cather had moved beyond an apprenticeship spent imitating Henry James before she created the pure, resonant prose we find in her major novels. Somehow, I feel called or chosen to tell this story. I now suspect that Cather's movement from silence into speech may have engrossed me because I wanted to move beyond my own silences. Like hers, they were not absences of language but language shaped for the approval of others. In writing her story, perhaps I could shape my own.
>
> My sense that I was writing something more limited and modest than a formal biography stemmed from my belief that I was not equal to that grand, noble, traditional art. If I ever attempted it, I was sure I would attract critical dismissals of my workmanlike efforts. I was also aware, although very faintly, of what I'd now call the power relationship between a biographer and her subject, a relationship that made me feel almost over-

whelmingly deferential to Cather. She was, after all, a famous American novelist, beloved by readers and praised by critics. I, on the other hand, was an obscure academic who had published a few articles in journals and anthologies. Who was I to think I could write a biography of Willa Cather?

I think, too, that even as I found the story of her literary emergence somehow nourishing, I was intimidated by what I could glean of Cather's personality from memoirs, letters and personal reminiscences. She was a strong, domineering woman who could be brutally dismissive of interfering literary upstarts. She was particularly annoyed by college professors who had the temerity to interpret her fiction and then—even worse—speculate about her life.

As a professor, I knew I was intimidated by the creative writer's disdain for scholars, but as a woman and a daughter I was also intimidated for a reason I did not then fully understand. For there is a certain kind of woman—powerful, self-involved, convinced of her own rightness and determined that her own views should prevail—who undermines my own sense of self more profoundly than the most patriarchal male.

I had met such a woman when I was an undergraduate [at Radcliffe]. She was a dean and my adviser. Armed with an impeccable private-school accent, she had beautifully coiffed white hair and dressed in elegantly tailored suits. I was an Irish Catholic graduate of a local public high school who was awed by the power of Harvard and Radcliffe, incarnated for me in my glacially perfect adviser. After I received my freshman midsemester grades—two B's and two C's, as I recall—she called me into her office and told me I was doing about as well as could be expected: "Those of you who were first in your high school class have just got to realize that you're competing with young women from more selective private schools. You'll graduate, but just don't expect to excel." The irony was that I had entered her office pleased with my grades; I had feared they would be worse. I left feeling annihilated.

Willa Cather reminded me of this woman. Her early journalism was scathing and self-assured, and her letters throughout her life were filled with pungent attacks and intense, unqualified approvals. In person, she could be compelling, and frightening. Elizabeth Sergeant, a close friend, recalled in *Willa Cather: A Memoir* what could happen when Cather was interrupted during her sacred morning working hours. One day an acquaintance who rang the bell, hoping to invite Cather to dinner that evening, was greeted with a "dark, dour face peering formidably over the banisters. *'Who are you, what do you want?'*" asked the face, causing the interloper to blush and stammer apologetically, reduced to the same state of powerless daughterhood in which the Radcliffe dean had placed me. . . .

I had reason to fear Cather's wrath. In writing about her, I was invading territory, both personal and literary, that she had wanted to keep private. Cather burned all the personal letters in her possession before she died, but I spent years traveling to libraries where remaining letters were kept, all the while knowing that restrictions on her estate forbade me from quoting from them. Thus as a biographer I was encountering not only a woman whose creative emergence was an uplifting story to me, but also a woman whose powerful voice and strong will could silence others, including future biographers. And behind Willa Cather stood other women who had reduced me to silence: a gargantuan gym teacher who considered me deficient in school spirit, a humorless nun whose creativity was channeled into spirit-breaking punishments, and, farther back, my own mother, whose interrogations always left me speechless.

The biographer's objectivity is a myth. Emotional and psy-

> chological currents that we do not fully understand draw us to our subjects; if we are lucky, we do not lose either ourselves or our subjects in the resulting whirlpool. In telling the story of Cather's creative emergence, I was honoring her personal and literary achievement. I would, I believed, help keep her work alive in the late 20th century, thus honoring her highest desire: that her fiction live and continue to be read.
>
> But I would also be doing something Cather did not want: I would be telling the story of her life from my point of view. In a way, I would also be rewriting one of the silencing stories of my own life, my domination by women who tried to erase me without ever seeing who I was. I was not aware of this impulse at the time, but I think now that my willingness to confront a literary figure whom I found threatening as well as engaging, and to articulate the truth about her as I saw it, helped release creative energies that sustained me through a very long project.[6]

O'Brien's own life thus becomes a story within a story. Books always are, even the most "objective."

Anthony Trollope arranged for his brief autobiography to be published after he died. It was, the following year, in 1883, and it scandalized Victorian England sufficiently that Trollope's immensely popular work fell out of popularity for the next hundred years. Trollope's scandal wasn't sexual, as it would have to be today. His scandal was simply to write candidly and honestly, as he says on the first page of his autobiography, about "the opening which a literary career offers to men and women for the earning of their bread."[7] The Victorians wanted noblesse oblige, not the simple truth. Trollope knew the quality of his work and felt no need to mystify it; he was proud of the *career* he'd made from an almost hopeless beginning and wanted to share his experience.

He celebrates his mother, understanding what a powerful example she had been for him. Here he recalls her when he was nineteen and living at home "without any idea of a career, or a profession, or a trade." She had him to support, a sick husband, one healthy and one frail daughter, and another son, with "a delicate chest":

> Now and again there would arise a feeling that it was hard upon my mother that she should have to do so much for us, that we should be idle while she was forced to work so constantly; but we should probably have thought more of that had she not taken to work as though it were the recognized condition of life for an old lady of fifty-five.
>
> Then, by degrees, an established sorrow was at home among us. My brother was an invalid, and the horrid word, which of all words were for some years after the most dreadful to us, had been pronounced. It was no longer a delicate chest, and some temporary necessity for peculiar care,—but consumption!* The Bruges doctor had said so, and we knew that he was right. From that time forth my mother's most visible occupation was that of nursing. There were two sick men in the house, and hers were the hands that tended them. The novels went on, of course. We had already learned to know that they would be forthcoming at stated intervals,—and they always were forthcoming. The doctor's vials and the ink-bottle held equal places in my mother's rooms. I have written many novels under many circumstances; but I doubt much whether I could write one when my whole heart was by the bedside of a dying son. Her power of dividing herself into two parts, and keeping her intellect by itself clear

* I.e., tuberculosis, the leading killer of the day. —R.R.

> from the troubles of the world, and fit for the duty it had to do, I never saw equalled. I do not think that the writing of a novel is the most difficult task which a man may be called upon to do; but it is a task that may be supposed to demand a spirit fairly at ease. The work of doing it with a troubled spirit killed Sir Walter Scott. My mother went through it unscathed in strength, though she performed all the work of day-nurse and night-nurse to a sick household;—for there were soon three of them dying.[8]

The third was Anthony's frail sister, also consumptive. In a short space of time, Mrs. Trollope lost a husband, a son, and a daughter, but she continued to turn out her books. Meanwhile Anthony went to work for the Post Office—employment arranged by a friend of his mother's—proved himself competent, was sent to Ireland as a district manager, and there, after some years of establishing himself, began to write. He had the advantage that comes to those who grow up in a craft or a profession—he knew what he was about:

> The vigor necessary to prosecute two professions at the same time is not given to every one, and it was only lately that I had found the vigor necessary for one. There must be early hours, and I had not as yet learned to love early hours. I was still, indeed, a young man; but hardly young enough to trust myself to find the power to alter the habits of my life. And I had heard of the difficulties of publishing. . . . I had dealt already with publishers on my mother's behalf, and knew that many a tyro who could fill a manuscript lacked the power to put his matter before the public;—and I knew, too, that when the matter was printed, how little had then been done towards the winning of the battle![9]

By "how little had then been done," I don't think Trollope is referring to finding no books in the stores on a book tour, but he may be.

Within a year he had written the first volume of a novel. He married—it was June 1844 by now and he was twenty-nine—and continued his Post Office work and his writing, and by 1845 he had finished his first novel. He passed it to his mother, "agreeing with her that it would be as well that she should not look at it before she gave it to a publisher," because "I knew that she did not give me credit for the sort of cleverness necessary for such work."[10] Whatever her estimate of her son's cleverness, Mrs. Trollope found him a publisher who was willing to publish the book and share the profits. But there were no profits, for some time to come: "More than twelve years had to pass . . . before I received any payment for any literary work which afforded an appreciable increase to our income."[11]

Trollope's reputation built slowly, as do the reputations of most writers; the best-selling first book is a rarity. *The Warden*, published in 1855, improved his public reception:

> The novel-reading world did not go mad about *The Warden;* but I soon felt that it had not failed as the others had failed. There were notices of it in the press, and I could discover that people around me knew that I had written a book. Mr. Longman [Trollope's publisher] was complimentary, and after a while informed me that there would be profits to divide. At the end of 1855 I received a cheque for £9 8s. 8d., which was the first money I had ever earned by literary work. . . . At the end of 1856 I received another sum of £10 15s. 1d. The pecuniary success was not great. Indeed, as regarded remuneration for the time, stone-breaking would have done better.[12]

But this stolid man was not to be denied. His writing procedure is famous:

> It was while I was engaged on *Barchester Towers* that I adopted a system of writing which, for some years afterwards, I found to be very serviceable to me. My time [as a Post Office official] was greatly occupied in traveling, and the nature of my traveling was now changed. I could not any longer do it on horseback. Railroads afforded me my means of conveyance, and I found that I passed in railway-carriages very many hours of my existence. Like others, I used to read. . . . But if I intended to make a profitable business out of my writing, and, at the same time, to do my best for the Post Office, I must turn these hours to more account than I could do even by reading. I made for myself therefore a little tablet, and found after a few days' exercise that I could write as quickly in a railway-carriage as I could at my desk. I worked with a pencil, and what I wrote my wife copied afterwards. In this way was composed the greater part of *Barchester Towers* and of the novel which succeeded it, and much also of others subsequent to them. My only objection to the practice came from the appearance of literary ostentation, to which I felt myself to be subject when going to work before four or five fellow-passengers. But I got used to it. . . .[13]

With *Barchester Towers,* Mr. Longman finally offered Trollope an advance, and that first substantial sum earned by his pen meant so much to the forty-two-year-old author that even at the end of his life he was quietly furious at those who scorn writing for money:

> I received my £100, in advance, with profound delight. It was a positive and most welcome increase in my income, and might probably be regarded as a first real step on the road to substantial success. I am well aware that there are many who think that an author in his authorship should not regard money,—nor a

painter, or sculptor, or composer in his art. I do not know that this unnatural sacrifice is supposed to extend itself further. A barrister, a clergyman, a doctor, an engineer, and even actors and architects, may without disgrace follow the bent of human nature, and endeavor to fill their bellies and clothe their backs, and also those of their wives and children, as comfortably as they can by the exercise of their abilities and their crafts. They may be as rationally realistic, as may the butchers and the bakers; but the artist and the author forget the high glories of their calling if they condescend to make a money return a first object. Those who preach this doctrine will be much offended by my theory.... They require the practice of a so-called virtue which is contrary to nature, and which, in my eyes, would be no virtue if it were practiced.... Did Titian or Rubens disregard their pecuniary rewards? As far as we know, Shakespeare worked always for money, giving the best of his intellect to support his trade as an actor. In our own century what literary names stand higher than those of Byron, Tennyson, Scott, Dickens, Macaulay, and Carlyle? And I think I may say that none of those great men neglected the pecuniary result of their labors.... It is a mistake to suppose that a man is a better man because he despises money. Few do so, and those few in doing so suffer a defeat. Who does not desire to be hospitable to his friends, generous to the poor, liberal to all, munificent to his children, and to be himself free from the carking fear which poverty creates? The subject will not stand an argument;—and yet authors are told that they should disregard payment for their work, and be content to devote their unbought brains to the welfare of the public. Brains that are unbought will never serve the public much. Take away from English authors their copyrights, and you would very soon take away from England her authors.[14]

What else can I say but Amen?

The work continued; the novels appeared as his mother's had appeared, year in, year out. Part of Trollope's autobiography is an extended essay, "On Novels and the Art of Writing Them," that I recommend to every beginning writer, whatever you intend to write. A paragraph on fictional characters samples the masterful whole:

> I am not sure that the construction of a perfected plot has been at any period within my power. But the novelist has other aims than the elucidation of his plot. He desires to make his readers so intimately acquainted with his characters that the creatures of his brain should be to them speaking, moving, living, human creatures. This he can never do unless he knows these fictitious personages himself, and he can never know them unless he can live with them in the full reality of established intimacy. They must be with him as he lies down to sleep, and as he wakes from his dreams. He must learn to hate them and to love them. He must argue with them, quarrel with them, forgive them, and even submit to them. He must know of them whether they be cold-blooded or passionate, whether true or false, and how far true, and how far false. The depth and the breadth, and the narrowness and the shallowness of each should be clear to him. And, as here, in our outer world, we know that men and women change,—become worse or better as temptation or conscience may guide them,—so should these creations of his change, and every change should be noted by him. On the last day of each month recorded, every person in his novel should be a month older than on the first. If the would-be novelist have aptitudes that way, all this will come to him without much struggling;—but if it do not come, I think he can only make novels of wood.[15]

Late in his autobiography, Trollope records his precise earnings from literary work across his entire lifetime, listing the return from each of his forty-six published works down to the last pence and totaling it all up: £68,939 17s. 5d., a munificent sum when the pound was worth five dollars and men worked for a dime a day. It was this bold accounting that poisoned his reputation with his peers.

Most of all, in Anthony Trollope's autobiographical *cri de coeur,* I cherish his indictment of the pernicious practice of waiting for "inspiration" to write. Why put your art at the mercy of your unconscious? Trollope had watched his mother work away come hell or high water and had duplicated her discipline in himself, and he knew better:

> I do not say that to all men has been given physical strength sufficient for such exertion as [mine], but I do believe that real exertion will enable most men to work at almost any season. I had previously to this arranged a system of task-work for myself, which I would strongly recommend to those who feel as I have felt, that labor, when not made absolutely obligatory by the circumstances of the hour, should never be allowed to become spasmodic. There was no day on which it was my positive duty to write for the publishers, as it was my duty to write reports for the Post Office. I was free to be idle if I pleased. But as I had made up my mind to undertake this second profession, I found it to be expedient to bind myself by certain self-imposed laws. When I have commenced a new book, I have always prepared a diary, divided into weeks, and carried it on for the period which I have allowed myself for the completion of the work. In this I have entered, day by day, the number of pages I have written, so that if at any time I have slipped into idleness for a day or two, the record of that idleness has been

there, staring me in the face, and demanding of me increased labor, so that the deficiency might be supplied. According to the circumstances of the time,—whether my other business might be then heavy or light, or whether the book which I was writing was or was not wanted with speed,—I have allotted myself so many pages a week. The average number has been about 40. It has been placed as low as 20, and has risen to 112. And as a page is an ambiguous term, my page has been made to contain 250 words; and as words, if not watched, will have a tendency to straggle, I have had every word counted as I went. In the bargains I have made with publishers I have,—not, of course, with their knowledge, but in my own mind,—undertaken always to supply them with so many words, and I have never put a book out of hand short of the number by a single word. I may also say that the excess has been very small. I have prided myself on completing my work exactly within the proposed dimensions.[*] But I have prided myself especially in completing it within the proposed time,—and I have always done so. There has ever been the record before me, and a week passed with an insufficient number of pages has been a blister to my eye, and a month so disgraced would have been a sorrow to my heart.

I have been told that such appliances are beneath the notice of a man of genius. I have never fancied myself to be a man of genius, but had I been so I think I might well have subjected myself to these trammels. Nothing surely is so potent as a law that may not be disobeyed. It has the force of the waterdrop that hollows the stone. A small daily task, if it be really daily, will beat the labors of a spasmodic Hercules.[†] It is the tortoise which always catches the hare. The hare has no chance. He

[*] Which is to say, Trollope wrote to length. —R.R.

[†] A page a day is a book a year. . . . —R.R.

loses more time in glorifying himself for a quick spurt than suffices for the tortoise to make half his journey.

I have known authors whose lives have always been troublesome and painful because their tasks have never been done in time. They have ever been as boys struggling to learn their lessons as they entered the school gates. Publishers have distrusted them, and they have failed to write their best because they have seldom written at ease. I have done double their work,—though burdened with another profession,—and have done it almost without effort. I have not once, throughout all my literary career, felt myself even in danger of being late with my task. I have known no anxiety as to "copy." The needed pages far ahead—very far ahead—have almost always been in the drawer beside me. And that little diary, with its dates and ruled spaces, its record that must be seen, its daily, weekly demand upon my industry, has done all that for me.

There are those who would be ashamed to subject themselves to such a taskmaster, and who think that the man who works with his imagination should allow himself to wait till—inspiration moves him. When I have heard such doctrines preached, I have hardly been able to repress my scorn. To me it would not be more absurd if the shoemaker were to wait for inspiration, or the tallow-chandler for the divine moment of melting. If the man whose business it is to write has eaten too many good things, or has drunk too much, or smoked too many cigars,—as men who write sometimes will do,—then his condition may be unfavorable for work; but so will be the condition of a shoemaker who has been similarly imprudent. I have sometimes thought that the inspiration wanted has been a remedy which time will give to the evil results of such imprudence. —*Mens sana in corpore sano.*[*] The

[*] "A sound mind in a sound body." —R.R.

> author wants that as does every other workman,—that and a habit of industry. I was once told that the surest aid to the writing of a book was a piece of cobbler's wax on my chair.* I certainly believe in the cobbler's wax much more than the inspiration.
>
> It will be said, perhaps, that a man whose work has risen to no higher pitch than mine has attained, has no right to speak of the strains and impulses to which real genius is exposed. I am ready to admit the great variations in brain power which are exhibited by the products of different men, and am not disposed to rank my own very high; but my own experience tells me that a man can always do the work for which his brain is fitted if he will give himself the habit of regarding his work as a normal condition of his life. I therefore venture to advise young men† who look forward to authorship as the business of their lives, even when they propose that that authorship be of the highest class known, to avoid enthusiastic rushes with their pens, and to seat themselves at their desks day by day as though they were lawyers' clerks;—and so let them sit until the allotted task shall be accomplished.[16]

Was Trollope a hack—a horse for hire? Mark Twain counted his words too; was he a hack? I think the answer is that both were professionals; imagine if a surgeon or a defense lawyer elected to wait for inspiration. But artists, having been mistaken for oracles, are excused from performance (and excuse themselves) on the grounds that the gods haven't incandesced them with mojo yet. Trollope was a great

* The Knickerbocker Rule! Was Knickerbocker paraphrasing Trollope? Who told Trollope? I'll bet his mother did. —R.R.

† Trollope's male chauvinism here is uncharacteristic; with his mother as exemplar, he portrayed strong, competent women in his fiction. He should have written "young men and young women." —R.R.

novelist. If you don't believe me, believe Tolstoy. When Tolstoy was working on *Anna Karenina,* he read Trollope to see how the doughty Englishman organized such fictions. Tolstoy reported his estimate of Anthony Trollope's quality in a note he left behind. "Trollope kills me," the author of *War and Peace* groaned, "kills me with his excellence!"[17]

You'll remember I suggested writing a profile of a fictional character if you had trouble fixing that character in your mind. For a last selection in this mini anthology of writers on writing, I offer what seems to be just such an exercise, by Sherwood Anderson. But it's more than that: it's the best demonstration I've seen of the mental process a writer goes through in quarrying from his preconscious the rough blocks of marble out of which he will fashion his book. A complete essay/story, untitled, that turned up among Anderson's papers after his death, it's worth every word:

> For a year now I have been thinking of writing a certain book. "Well, tomorrow I'll get at it," I've been saying to myself. Every night when I get into bed, I think about the book. The people that are to be put between its covers dance before my eyes. I live in the city of Chicago, and at night motor trucks go rumbling along the roadway outside my house. Not so very far away there is an elevated railroad, and after 12 o'clock at night trains pass at pretty long intervals. Before it began I went to sleep during one of the quiet intervals, but now that the idea of writing this book has got into me I lie awake and think.
>
> For one thing, it is hard to get the whole idea of the book fixed in the setting of the city I live in now. I wonder if you, who do not try to write books, perhaps will understand what I mean. Maybe you will, maybe you won't. It is a little hard to

explain. You see, it's something like this. You as a reader will, some evening or some afternoon, be reading in my book and then you will grow tired of reading and put it down. You will go out of your house and into the street. The sun is shining and you meet people you know. There are certain facts of your life just the same as of mine. If you are a man, you go from your house to an office and sit at a desk where you pick up a telephone and begin to talk about some matter of business with a client or a customer of your house. If you are an honest housewife, the iceman has come, or there drifts into your mind the thought that yesterday you forgot to remember some detail concerned with running your house. Little outside thoughts come and go in your mind, and it is so with me too. For example, when I have written the above sentence, I wonder why I have written the words "honest housewife." A housewife, I suppose, can be as dishonest as I can. What I am trying to make clear is that, as a writer, I am up against the same things that confront you, as a reader.

What I want to do is to express in my book a sense of the strangeness that has gradually, since I was a boy, been creeping more and more into my feeling about everyday life. It would all be very simple if I could write of life in an interior city of China or in an African forest. A man I know has recently told me of another man who, wanting to write a book about Parisian life and having no money to go to Paris to study the life there, went instead to the city of New Orleans. He had heard that many people lived in New Orleans whose ancestors were French. "They will have retained enough of the flavor of Parisian life for me to get the feeling," he said to himself. The man told me that the book turned out to be very successful and that the city of Paris read with delight a translation of his work as a study of French life, and I am only sorry I can't find as simple a way out of my own job.

The whole point with me is that my wish to write this book springs from a somewhat different notion. "If I can write everything out plainly, perhaps I will myself understand better what has happened," I say to myself and smile. During these days I spend a good deal of time smiling at nothing. It bothers people. "What are you smiling about now?" they ask, and I am up against as hard a job trying to answer as I am trying to get under way with my book.

Sometimes in the morning I sit down at my desk and begin writing, taking as my subject a scene from my own boyhood. Very well, I am coming home from school. The town in which I was born and raised was a dreary, lonely little place in the far western section of the state of Nebraska, and I imagine myself walking along one of its streets. Sitting upon a curbing before a store is a sheepherder who has left his flock many miles away in the foothills at the base of the western mountains and has come into our town, for what purpose he himself does not seem to know. He is a bearded man without a hat and sits with his mouth slightly open, staring up and down the street. There is a half-wild, uncertain look in his eyes, and his eyes have awakened a creepy feeling in me. I hurry away with a kind of dread of some unknown thing eating at my vital organs. Old men are great talkers. It may be that only kids know the real terror of loneliness.

I have tried, you see, to start my book at that particular point in my own life. "If I can catch exactly the feeling of that afternoon of my boyhood, I can give the reader the key to my character," I tell myself.

The plan won't work. When I have written 5, 10, 1,500 words, I stop writing and look out my window. A man is driving a team of horses hitched to a wagonload of coal along my street and is swearing at another man who drives a Ford. They have both stopped and are cursing each other. The coal wagon driver's face is black with coal dust, but anger has reddened his cheeks and the red and black have produced a dusky brown like the skin of a Negro.

I have got up from my typewriter and walk up and down in my room, smoking cigarettes. My fingers pick up little things on my desk and then put them down.

I am nervous like the race horses I used to be with at one period of my boyhood. Before a race and when they had been brought out on the tracks before all the people and before the race started, their legs quivered. Sometimes there was a horse got into such a state that when the race started, he would do nothing. "Look at him. He can't untrack himself," we said.

Right now I am in that state about my book. I run to the typewriter, write for a time and then walk nervously about. I smoke a whole package of cigarettes during the morning.

And then suddenly I have again torn up all I have written. "It won't do," I have told myself.

In this book I am not intending to try to give you the story of my life. "What of life, any man's life?—forked radishes running about, writing declarations of independence, telling themselves little lies, having dreams, getting puffed up now and then with what is called greatness. Life begins, runs its course and ends," a man I once knew told me one evening, and it is true. Even as I write these words, a hearse is going through my street. Two young girls, who are going off with two young men to walk, I suppose, in the fields where the city ends, stop laughing for a moment and look up at the hearse. It will be a moment before they forget the passing hearse and begin laughing again.

"A life is like that, it passes like that," I say to myself as I tear up my sheets and begin again walking and smoking the cigarettes.

If you think I am sad, having these thoughts about the brevity and insignificance of a life, you are mistaken. In the state I am in, such things do not matter. "Certain things last," I say to myself. "One might make things a little clear. One might even imagine a man, say a Negro, going along a city street and humming a song. It catches the ear of another man, who repeats it on the next day. A thin strand of song, like a tiny stream far up in some hill, begins to flow down into the wide plains. It waters the fields. It freshens the air above a hot stuffy city."

Now I have got myself worked up into a state. I am always doing that these days. I write again, and again tear up my words.

I go out of my room and walk about.

I have been with a woman I have found and who loves me. It has happened that I am a man who has not been loved by women and have all my life been awkward and a little mixed up when in their presence. Perhaps I have had too much respect for them, have wanted them too much. That may be. Anyway, I am not so rattled in her presence.

She, I think, has a certain control over herself, and that is helpful to me. When I am with her I keep smiling to myself and thinking, "It would be rather a joke all around if she found me out."

When she is looking in another direction, I study her a little. That she should seem to like me so much surprises me, and I am sore at my own surprise. I grow humble and do not like my humbleness either. "What is she up to? She is very lovely. Why is she wasting her time with me?"

I shall remember always certain hours when I have been with her. Late on a certain Sunday afternoon, I remember. I sat in a chair in a room in her apartment. I sat with my hand against my cheek, leaning a little forward. I had dressed myself carefully because I was going to see her, had put on my best suit of clothes. My hair was carefully combed and my glasses carefully balanced on my rather large nose.

And there I was, in her apartment in a certain city, in a chair in a rather dark corner, with my hand against my cheek, looking as solemn as an old owl. We had been walking about and had come into the house and she had gone away, leaving me sitting there, as I have said. The apartment was in a part of the city where many foreign people live, and from my chair I could, by turning my head a little, look down into a street filled with Italians.

It was growing dark outside, and I could just see the people in the street. If I cannot remember facts about my own and other people's lives, I can always remember every feeling that has gone through me, or that I have thought went through anyone about me.

The men going along the street below the window all had dark, swarthy faces and nearly all of them wore, somewhere about them, a spot of color. The younger men, who walked with a certain swagger, all had on flaming red ties. The street was dark, but far down the street there was a spot where a streak of sunlight still managed to find its way in between two tall buildings and fell sharp against the face of a smaller red-brick building. It pleased my fancy to imagine the street had also put on a red necktie, perhaps because there would be love-making along the street before Monday morning.

Anyway, I sat there looking and thinking such thoughts as came to me. The women who went along the street nearly all had dark-colored shawls drawn up about their faces. The roadway was filled with children whose voices made a sharp tinkling sound.

My fancy went out of my body in a way of speaking, I suppose, and I began thinking of myself as being at that moment in a city in Italy. Americans like myself who have not traveled are always doing that. I suppose the people of another nation would not understand how doing it is almost a necessity in our lives, but any American will understand. The American, particularly a Middle American, sits as I was doing at that moment, dreaming, you understand, and suddenly he is in Italy or in a Spanish town where a dark-looking man is riding a bony horse along a street, or he is being driven over the Russian steppes in a sled by a man whose face is all covered with whiskers. It is an idea of the Russians got from looking at cartoons in newspapers, but it answers the purpose. In the distance, a pack of wolves are following the sled. A fellow I once knew told me that Americans are always up to such tricks because all of our old stories and dreams have come to us from over the sea and because we have no old stories and dreams of our own.

Of that I can't say. I am not putting myself forward as a thinker on the subject of the causes of the characteristics of the American people or any other monstrous or important matter of that kind.

But anyway, there I was, sitting, as I have told you, in the Italian section of an American city and dreaming of myself being in Italy.

To be sure, I wasn't alone. Such a fellow as myself never is alone in his dreams. And as I said having my dream, the woman with whom I had been spending the afternoon, and with whom I am no doubt what is called "in love," passed between me and the window through which I had been looking. She had on a dress of some soft clinging stuff, and her slender figure made a very lovely line across the light. Well, she was like a young tree you might see on a hill, in a windstorm perhaps.

What I did, as you may have supposed, was to take her with me into Italy.

The woman became at once, and in my dream, a very beautiful princess in a strange land I have never visited. It may be that when I was a boy in my Western town some traveler came there to lecture on life in Italian cities before a club that met at the Presbyterian church and to which my mother belonged, or perhaps later I read some novel the name of which I can't remember.

And so my princess had come down to me along a path out of a green wooded hill where her castle was located. She had walked under blossoming trees in the uncertain evening light, and some blossoms had fallen on her black hair. The perfume of Italian nights was in her hair. That notion came into my head. That's what I mean.

What really happened was that she saw me sitting there lost in my dream and, coming to me, rumpled my hair and upset the glasses perched on my big nose and, having done that, went laughing out of the room.

I speak of all this because later, on that same evening, I lost all notion of the book I am now writing and sat until 3 in the morning, writing on another book, making the woman the central figure. "It will be a story of old times, filled with moons and stars and the fragrance of half-decayed trees in an old land," I told myself, but when I had written many pages, I tore them up too.

"Something has happened to me or I should not be filled with the idea of writing this book at all," I told myself, going to my window to look out at the night. "At a certain hour of a

> certain day and in a certain place, something happened that has changed the whole current of my life.
>
> "The thing to be done," I then told myself, "is to begin writing my book by telling as clearly as I can the adventures of that certain moment."[18]

Anderson's narrative of getting started is like a fugue, isn't it, themes appearing and being picked up, inverted, augmented, transformed. It's like my writing twenty draft chapters before I worked out how to tell the story that became *The Last Safari*. There's no such thing as a cookbook for writing. If you didn't know that when you opened this little book of mine, I'm sure you know it by now. Writing is always like scuba diving, a descent as deep as you can or dare to go, given your capacity and your level of skill, into a medium that grades from emerald clarity into fathomless darkness and propagates out and on deeper and farther than you or anyone or all of us together can ever dive. "The sea water glows around our bodies as we move," I wrote after my month in the Everglades and along the Gulf shore:

> night plankton: they come alive with the light in the moving water we make, dots, sparkles, flashes, flares. We stare under water at a flood of stars glowing around the tips of our fingers, lighting our kicking feet and our stroking arms. They were here all along in the bright day and we did not know. We swirl them into light and they decorate us, imitating the stars above, microscopic things glowing in the water like the giant stars reduced by incomprehensible distances to points of white in the black sky. The stars in the sky and night plankton making stars in the water wherever we go: layers, and layers under layers down into the very center of things, and layers there too small to see, and layers below those layers until the head swims and

> still more layers then. We are no more divided from the world than the water itself is divided. When we damage the world we damage ourselves. If we destroy it we destroy ourselves. A piece at a time, we think, a part at a time, but the world has no pieces and does not come apart. Wherever we put our hands, points of energy trail off from us like the tails of comets. The tree that falls without sound falls within our hearing.[19]

Writing goes everywhere. How wonderful that it should.

Ten

BOTTOM

A few more stories, a few more ideas to share, and then we're done. One perverse proof that writing is a craft is the limited number of general statements you can make about it. Books on how to write are short because writing is local and specific, hands on, the product of unique problems solved one at a time. Lectures don't take you very far. You have to learn by apprenticeship.

You can apprentice to living writers in writing programs, an approach that has the advantage of interaction and of the emotional support that comes from finding a mentor. You can and should also learn from writers who left their works behind to be studied not only for their finish but also for their characteristic chisel marks. Biographies often supply information about how writers worked, how they solved writing problems. Variorum editions of stories and poems can show you the creative process in action, as I tried to demonstrate in my essay on reference books.

The English use a homely word, "bottom," to refer to the qualities of physical and psychic endurance that Americans and Germans mean when they talk of "willpower" or "will." Racehorses that stay the course have "bottom"; so do boxers who get up and go on fighting after they're knocked down. Emerson alludes to this quality in *English*

Traits: "Broad-bottomed, broad-fronted Saxons," he praises the English, "they stand foursquare astride the world." I like the word especially because it corporealizes the Knickerbocker Rule. Trollope's adviser would adhere it with cobbler's wax. Americans similarly invoke cement when they recommend "stick-to-itiveness." Writers need to cultivate bottom within each work of writing—and across a career of writing as well (it's intrinsically a valuable quality anyway). My endorsement isn't merely cheerleading. Emotional continuity is vital to a work of writing. Bottom sustains that continuity.

Good books feel all of a piece. They communicate a sense of unity as you read them, and you remember them as a unity afterward. That's why the reviewers' complaints that *Moby-Dick* and *Ulysses* were "middens"—loose, disordered accumulations—said more about their ear than about the books: because an unprejudiced reading (now that the shock of the new has discharged) conveys a convincing sense of their unity even though each story is told in different and multiple voices.

It isn't easy to sustain emotional continuity across a work, particularly a long work. Melville wrote *Moby-Dick* intensely, in a relatively short period of time, ignoring the noontime meals his wife set outside his study door, sometimes stumbling in the street from exhaustion after a day's work. Under such circumstances—Solzhenitsyn wrote *The Gulag Archipelago* the same way, as a cathartic unburdening—emotional continuity is more or less guaranteed. But Joyce wrote and rewrote *Ulysses* across a space of five years. His previous book, *A Portrait of the Artist as a Young Man,* took twelve years. Joyce had bottom.

Voice is important at the technical level to sustain continuity in work that's protracted or delayed. Voice is a role you put on, as an actor puts on a role when he steps out onto the stage. Once you've found a way to tell a particular story and have exercised that voice long enough to know how to sustain its tone, you can usually activate it again after an interruption by rereading what you wrote before. That's one reason why you should become conscious of voice in writing and make deliberate decisions about it rather than organize it intuitively. If you've created a voice deliberately—if you know who's telling the story—you'll have a better chance of sustaining that voice than if you've left it to unconscious processes; unconscious production can be fugitive.

But there's something else behind voice, something personal and private, that makes it possible to sustain continuity in a work. Most of us sustain continuity within ourselves—continuity of identity—automatically, as automatically as we balance ourselves walking, by a kind of psychic homeostasis. Sometimes—usually when we're hit with emotional or cultural shocks—we have to intervene in the process more consciously. By grieving, by introspecting, through dark nights of the soul and new days dawning, we incorporate the unsettling experiences and reassemble ourselves. Sustaining continuity in a work requires the same strategies as sustaining continuity within yourself.

Many of the people Ginger and I have interviewed who survived severe child abuse tell similar stories of hiding their essential self and protecting that self against the assaults of their abusers, preserving it for survival (soul murder, the psychoanalyst Leonard Shengold calls the terrible assault on identity that the most destructive abusers inflict). One young woman we interviewed remembered vividly the exact moment in childhood when her mother was beating her when she decided not to split into multiple personalities. Significantly, she decided not to fragment her identity because she knew, even at twelve years of age, that she had to survive in one piece to tell the story of her abuse. Viktor Frankl found a similar drive toward survival in Auschwitz and Dachau, correspondingly linked to finding a purpose worth surviving for. You need bottom to sustain identity against the mutability of life; you need bottom similarly to sustain writing a book.

On the other hand, don't go asking for trouble. There's an old rule that says you should try not to make major life changes while you're in psychotherapy. The principle applies to writing as well.

Patience is a significant component of bottom; it may be the most important single quality a writer needs to cultivate. From the book in your head, a wheat field ripe with grain, you have to gather and process the real book you'll write, milling and mixing and extruding the story out through a grinding plate in a thin string of words. Some people try to write first drafts in one exhausting squirt at full pressure, racing to get the words down before they lose their elusive sense of the whole. They work night and day and hardly eat or sleep. If you have to work that way, do, but it's possible to learn to hold everything in your head and work forward patiently, shaping the draft more carefully as you go. Trollope was such a master of patient craftsmanship that he not only wrote his books in one finished draft with very little revision but also started writing a new book immediately upon finishing the last—which means he held more than one book in his head at a time.

Sometimes it's impossible to race-draft a book. I had too much information to process to write *The Making of the Atomic Bomb* that way. Racing through a first draft looks to me like writing on a computer without backing up your file; if the power goes out—if life interrupts the drafting process, as it often does—you could lose the book. People race through first drafts partly because they sense that a more deliberate pace would result in a different book. They're right, of course; it probably would. But the book you write is only one of the many possible books that might have led off from your original conception. Whether a book you compose deliberately will be not merely different from but also inferior to a book you race-draft is a decision you'll have to make. I've written books both ways and both ways worked. I race-drafted when I was learning how to organize books; now I compose more deliberately.

Everyone has to sleep, so you're always interrupted when you write. Many writers have a serious problem shutting off writing at the end of the day and turning it on again the next morning. One consequence can be insomnia, which is ultimately self-defeating. Writers who use alcohol to shut themselves down at the end of the day risk hangover or worse; heavy drinking damages short-term memory—exactly the kind of memory you need to juggle words and sentences and evoke associations as you write. I quit using alcohol years ago, partly for that reason. I get up at 7 A.M. I'm at my desk by eight-thirty nearly every morning when I'm writing, after coffee and the *New York Times.* I write until eleven-thirty; I break for lunch; I'm back at my desk by one-thirty; I stop no later than six. After dinner Ginger and I usually channel-surf until eight-thirty or nine and then go to bed and read. My evening reading is almost always related to the writing I'm doing. On this comfortable schedule, once I get a book started, I usually write from five to ten pages a day, five days a week—a chapter a week. It takes me about an hour of doing other things at the end of the day to disconnect from writing—fixing dinner, bicycling, watering the fruit trees I'm trying to grow despite the voracious Connecticut deer. If a phrase or an idea pops into mind I grab a three-by-five and write it down. Sometimes, when I'm writing, the head of pressure is such that I wake in the middle of the night or early in the morning with whole scenes boiling up that demand to be recorded. Then I stagger into my office rubbing my eyes, move the jar of Blackwings within reach on my desk, and write by hand on a yellow tablet until the pressure abates. If it's still night I go back to bed; if it's morning I shower, go about my day, and catch a nap nodding in front of my computer after lunch.

You can learn to shut off the flow at the end of the day. You write in a state of dissociation, your consciousness split and multiplied; dissociation yields to activities that calm or distract. Physical activity works best for me, physical activity or domestic duties. I go into a mindless state for a while and emerge myself again, with the writing running quietly on idle in the background until tomorrow.

To start up again in the morning, if the engine isn't already racing, I usually reread what I wrote the day before. That exercise can be hazardous; it can lead you off into editing and rewriting when you want to be composing new material. I've started rereading, let myself become distracted with editing, and found the morning gone with no new pages composed. As a result, I try to separate formal editing from composition, although there's always informal editing to do along the way, particularly decisions about word choice.

Documents and artifacts can help you start up after an interruption. I try to bring home not only documents and photographs but also physical artifacts when I'm traveling for research, to engage more of my senses as I write. A piece of granite I collected at twelve thousand feet in the Swiss Alps powerfully recalls that snow-glared, breathless afternoon. A handful of grain heads smells and susurrates like a wheat field. When I visited Donner State Park I shot 360 degrees of overlapping photographs of the surrounding mountains. I had the prints enlarged, cut them out, and taped them together around the wall of my office to give me a view comparable to the Donners'.

Sometimes, after an interruption or some other event, you discover that the book you're writing has gone dead on the page—that you've lost your emotional connection to the story and don't feel the words when you reread them. Such disconnection is common in the last stages of writing, when you've reread the words so often that your eyes glide over them and your mind is elsewhere. The remedy to overfamiliarity, as I said earlier, is either to age the book for a while on the shelf or to concentrate harder.

If the writing has gone dead earlier in the course of composition, however, you may have a serious problem. It may be a problem with voice and point of view, like the difficulty I had writing the opening chapter of *The Last Safari*, in which case it should resolve itself if you beat your head against the wall long enough. Or it may be a symptom of deeper distress. Sometimes your psyche won't let you write a book that's wrong for you, as sometimes your psyche won't let you love someone you think you ought to love. Leo Szilard's parents expected their son to study engineering, not theoretical physics. He dutifully complied but found himself increasingly unable to listen to engineering lectures. "In the end, as always," he recalled late in life, "the subconscious proved stronger than the conscious and made it impossible to make any progress in my studies of engineering."[1] He left the engineering school where he was studying and enrolled in physics at the University of Berlin; within a year he had made a major discovery. Sometimes writers have to give up writing a particular book, temporarily or finally, because the book isn't working. I had that experience with the novel I wrote during my Guggenheim Fellowship year, and it was traumatic. Other than the obvious recommendation—that you think and feel your project through as thoroughly as possible before you commit to it—I don't know how to avoid such experiences; they're part of the human condition. If it's any consolation, they usually signal a major spurt of emotional growth.

You need bottom to persevere in writing. It's difficult work, and you can't fully master it at school. Even now, all these books and articles later, writing often feels to me like groping in darkness along a wall. It should; it's sensory thought pushed through an abstract transformation, and no one ever said thinking of any kind was easy. Hardly anyone will credit you when you decide to go about it. "Writing was a curveball that I never saw coming," writes Larry Brown, the Mississippi fireman. "It's such an improbable and foolish-sounding thing to say in front of anybody: 'I'm going to become a writer. I'm going to learn how to write a book.' "[2] Most writers take it up because they can't *not* do it; they write because they have to. Don't let anyone talk you out of it. It's your language, your story, your life.

Story enlightens us. All of us, not only writers. Story is the primary vehicle human beings use to structure knowledge and experience. The molecular biologist Robert Pollack, in *Signs of Life,* identifies DNA as a text, the basis for a story:

> Evolution has taken about four billion years to write the set of texts we can find in the DNA of creatures alive today. We are about to be able to read them in much the same manner we read any book of our own creating.... Nor is there really any choice in the matter: once we begin to read the book that describes how we ourselves are made, it is unlikely we will stop in the middle....[3]

> One of the best definitions of literature comes from the Italian novelist Italo Calvino; in his *Six Memos for the Next Millennium,* Calvino tried to characterize the essence of great literature. His prescription for the literature of the twenty-first century included five qualities: lightness, quickness, exactitude, visibility, and multiplicity. As it happens, the genome of a person has all of these qualities in abundance. It is light because it is as small as the rigors of natural selection permit. It is quick because it must be: the life of a cell is short, and the entire text of the genome must be copied in a few hours; in the case of an embryo, the genomic text must make a person ready for the world—starting from a single cell—in only a few months. It is exact because its base sequences and the proteins they encode create the specificity of surfaces that gives living things their distinctive complexity and efficiency in a disordered universe. It is visible because cells, the genome's readers, assemble it into living things from its instructions. But above all, the human genome is multiple. We are different from one another, and this allows the DNA texts within us to carry the infinite multiplicity of possibility in human character, and, most especially, in the hopes we have for our children.[4]

Another scientist, the distinguished Harvard entomologist Edward O. Wilson, recalls in his autobiography, *Naturalist,* how he came to identify the biological basis for dominance, the displacement of endemic local species by interlopers from outside, an important discovery:

> More precisely, what hereditary traits caused an assemblage of species to spread into new lands and overwhelm the old endemics? The surrender of any group is all the more puzzling because endemics have had thousands or millions of years to become adapted to the habitats they occupy before the invaders appear.
>
> This problem of the biological cause of dominance was not clear in my mind as I began my own biogeographic study, a monograph on the ants of New Guinea and surrounding regions. But [previous researchers], who never asked the question directly themselves, had primed me to formulate it. All I needed, I realize in retrospect today, was a small set of data to fall into place in order for the question to form somewhere in my subconscious. Then, driven by the power of the mythic conqueror archetype evoked by [the previous researchers], I would put together a tentative scenario, a story, and a phrase to capture it all. . . .[5]

"A pattern did emerge," Wilson comments. ". . . Evolutionary biology always yields patterns if you look hard enough, because there are a hundred parameters and a thousand patterns, awaiting examination."[6] Human experience, one subset of evolutionary biology, also yields patterns; and scientists and other storytellers, even you and I, shape them into stories.

I offer examples from science because science is what I read. They have the advantage of demonstrating the universality of story in our lives and they help explain the impulse to write: we write to discover the patterns, Pollack's "infinite multiplicity of possibility in human character," to understand ourselves, to identify and celebrate what we have in common, to assure that we are not alone.

The Yale psychologist Robert Sternberg finds story at the center of the human behavior we call love. "Love is a story," he told the reporter Bruce Fellman, "a story each of us is constantly writing and rewriting. Love develops, grows, and lasts when a person finds someone else who fits what his or her particular story is all about."[7] Sternberg studies intelligence and believes loving to be one kind. Fellman explains:

> "The story is who you are," says Sternberg, adding that such lifetime tales are crafted from a wide variety of disparate elements: family experiences, religion, school, watching television and movies, reading, culture in general, and time in the back seat, to name some of the more obvious inputs. "And it's never completed," he says. "Your personal story is very dynamic."
>
> Although everyone's personal narrative is as individual as a fingerprint, Sternberg . . . has learned that the tales can be grouped into roughly two dozen fundamental categories. Along with the hearts-and-flowers romance, there is what he calls the police story, the mystery, the gardening tale, and the pornographic essay. There are humorous stories, with one partner cast as Johnny Carson and the other playing Ed McMahon, and there are science fiction thrillers in which the plot line calls for a person to team up with someone who seems to be as incomprehensible and strange as an alien from another planet. . . .
>
> "You have to know your own story," [Sternberg] says, "and it has to mesh with your partner's story. . . . Stories are of great interest to psychologists because they can predict, explain, and help us understand what people will do and why they do it."[8]

Story is necessary to life. Jonathan Shay implies such a necessity when he identifies the "cohesion of consciousness" with the ability to create "fully realized narrative." The Vietnam veterans whom Shay treats come to him stuck in a perpetual present, cycling repeatedly through the horrors they experienced, unable to retreat or advance. Not only love is a story; our entire lives are stories that we tell ourselves and each other.

Artists and writers produce creative works on an intuitive internal schedule; when creative production ceases, so, usually, does life. This remarkable discovery belongs to the Italian physicist Cesare Marchetti. Marchetti fitted the cumulative production of creative works by various recognized geniuses through history to what mathematicians call a logistic curve, an S-shaped curve of natural growth such as all natural systems follow:

THE GROWTH OF A BACTERIA COLONY[9]

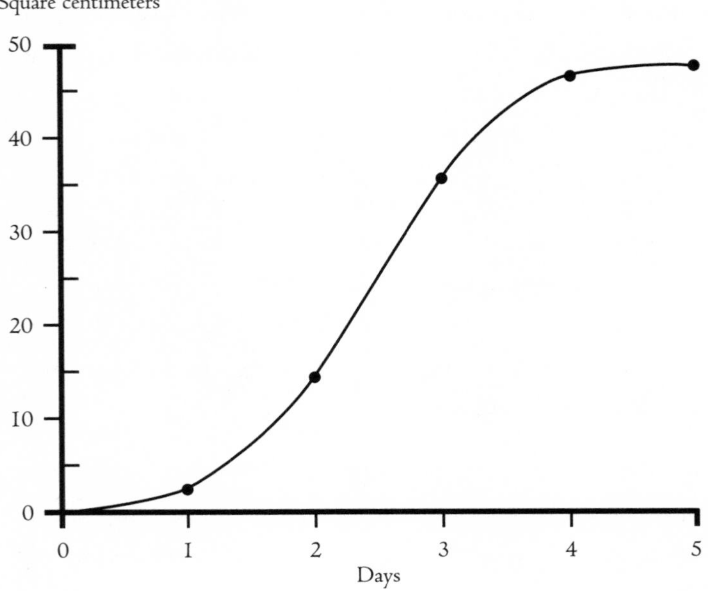

The rate of growth of anything living—a newborn child, an epidemic disease, a population of rabbits or bacteria in an enclosed area—is proportional to both how much growth has already occurred and how much growth can follow. Early and late in the game these quantities are small, and therefore the rate of growth is small. "The rate is greatest in the middle," writes the physicist Theodore Modis, explaining Marchetti's discovery, "where both the growth accomplished and the growth remaining are sizable."[10] These differences in rate of growth generate a characteristic S-shaped curve.

> Cesare Marchetti [writes Modis] was the first to associate the evolution of a person's creativity and productivity with natural growth. . . . He . . . proceeded to study hundreds of well-documented artists and scientists. In each case he took the total number of creations known for each of these people, graphed them over time, and determined the S-curve that would best connect the data points. He found that most people died close to having realized their perceived potential. In his words:
>
> > To illustrate further what I mean by the perceived potential, consider the amount of beans a man has in his bag and the amount left when he finally dies. Looking at the cases mentioned here . . . I find that the leftover beans are usually 5 to 10 percent of the total. Apparently when Mozart died at thirty-five years of age, he had already said what he had to say.
>
> The idea is intriguing. Obviously, people's productivity increases and decreases with time. Youngsters cannot produce much because they have to learn first. Old people may

become exhausted of ideas, energy, and motivation. It makes intuitive sense that one's productivity goes through a life cycle over one's lifetime, slowing down as it approaches the end.[11]

Modis decided to check Marchetti's theory for himself. He looked up the record of Mozart's work and found the logistic curve that best fit:

WOLFGANG AMADEUS MOZART (1756–1791)[12]

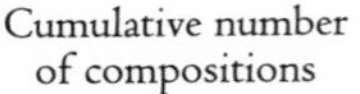

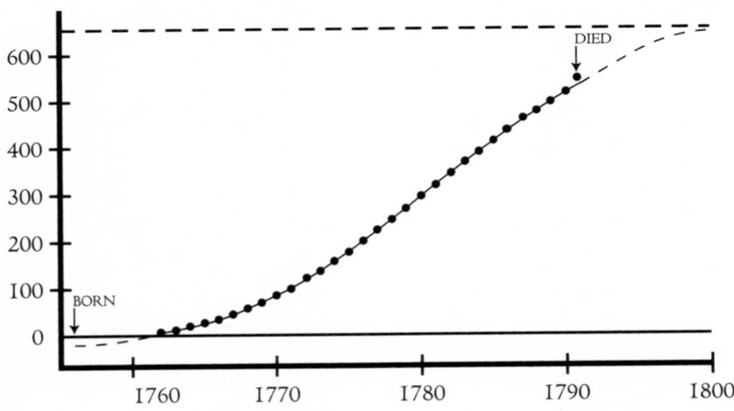

"In discussions with musicians," Modis adds, "I have found that many are not shocked by the idea that Mozart may have exhausted his creative potential at the age of thirty-five. He had already contributed so much in every musical form of the time that he probably could have added little more in another fifty years of calendar time. He himself wrote at the age of twenty-one: 'To live until one can no longer contribute anything new to music.' "[13]

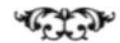

Ernest Hemingway appears to have exhausted his creative potential by the time he killed himself, so that, Modis notes, "it was a natural time for him to die, even though he took his own life."[14]

ERNEST HEMINGWAY (1899–1961)[15]

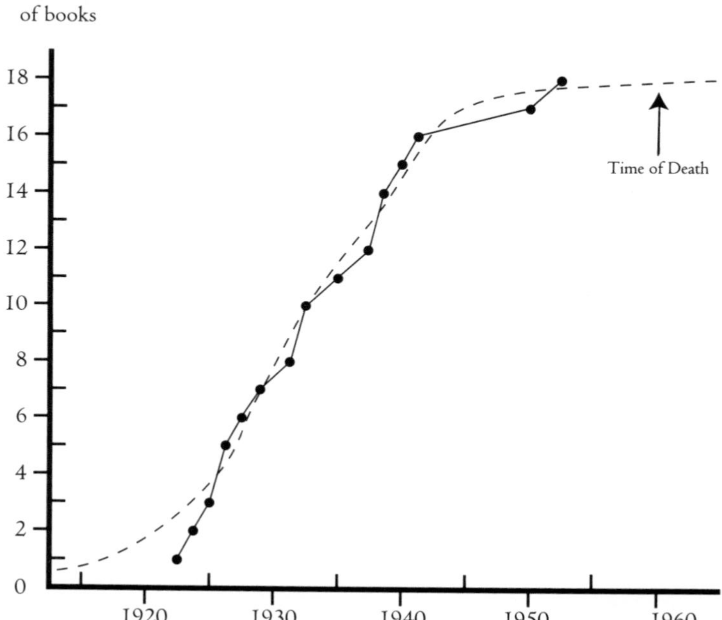

Modis overlooks a point about Hemingway's productivity that the logistic curve makes clear and that Hemingway's biographers have confirmed: the novelist stopped producing ten years before he died, a drying up of creativity that contributed significantly to his decision to end his life.

Percy Bysshe Shelley, on the other hand, who drowned at thirty in a sailing accident, might have produced twice the number of poems he left behind had he lived; his death was truly unnatural:

PERCY BYSSHE SHELLEY (1792–1822)[16]

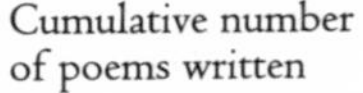

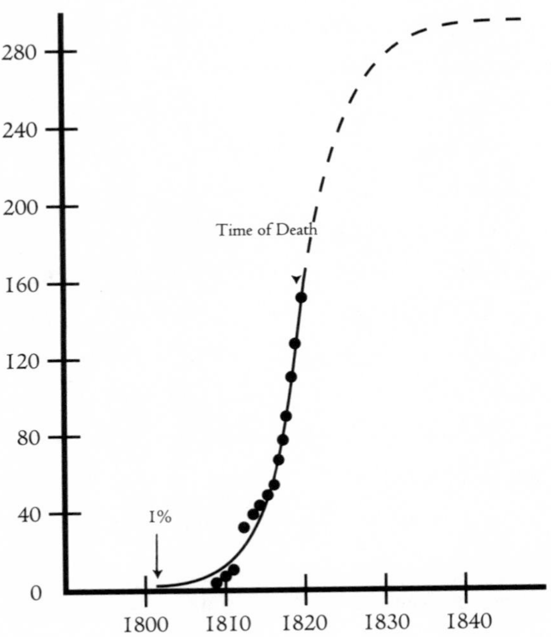

Marchetti's and Modis's growth-curve studies are not hocus-pocus. They're demonstrations of underlying patterns. They imply that each of us has a potential in life that, barring accident, we literally live to fulfill.

Earlier I discussed the complexities of beginning a work of writing. Middles are middles, one foot in front of the other. Now we come to the end. "The same iron rigor needed to begin the book is required to end it," says Gabriel García Márquez. At the beginning you anchor lines of story, characters, theme, plots, and subplots. In the middle you extend them, loop them around, run them through various rings. At the end you tie them all together. Characters, story, theme, plots, and subplots come to their appropriate resolution. Everything has changed because of what happened in the course of your story; your story has moved from one place to another; the characters who fell into a hole now climb back out. I find endings go much more quickly than beginnings, because I know where the lines run and I've thought along the way about how I want to tie them up.

Realistic writers scoff at the O. Henry ending, the trick at the end that reverses the thrust of the story. That's because an O. Henry ending mechanically subverts the story that came before and the continuity of character of the characters within it. Naive readers enjoy such endings, which are modeled on fairy tales and have affinities with magic and with gambling, two other arenas where abrupt transformations are commonplace. But some people do win lotteries and jackpots; an O. Henry ending isn't out of place in verity if you can document it.

Stories begin either *ab ovo,* from the beginning, or *in medias res,* in the middle of the action, but no one seems to have defined corresponding terms for the way stories end. Traditional endings tie up all the lines out in the open. Classical comedies end with a wedding banquet, signifying the reuniting of the community and promising its continuation. Classical tragedies end with a scene of revelation where the tragic central figure finally understands his hubris; the resolution of the tragedy takes place somewhere beyond the ending—on the other side of the stage, as it were, says Northrop Frye—where the community has been purified of its disorder. In either case, we know what happened. A good term for the traditional ending, following from *ab ovo,* might be *ad finis:* to the end.

The modern style in fiction—Hemingway's novels, for example—rejects tying up the lines in the open, perhaps because doing so has come to seem too old-fashioned and mechanical, perhaps because the modern style rejects omniscience, with its implication that the world is orderly and predictable. Modern novelists appear to have modeled their characteristic ending on the short story, which has neither beginning nor end but only a subtle shifting of terms somewhere along the way like the fulcrum that breaks a poem into statement and resolution. (Robert Frost: "The old dog barks backward without getting up./ I can remember when he was a pup.")[17] Since novels do have beginnings and ends, the modern style can't reproduce the short-story ending but has to imitate it. What in fact happens is that the writer approaches the end of his novel knowing how the lines tie up but cuts the end across the lines rather than extending the story out to its conclusion. Since cutting across the story is how stories start that don't start *ab ovo,* the modern ending turns out to be another application of the ancient device of *in medias res.* So stories may begin and end in the middle of the action, like a sausage with the two crimped ends chopped off.

I found I needed no fewer than three endings to close out *The Ungodly*. The first ending closed out the main tale (it also happens to be true). Lewis Keseberg, the monster of the story, having (in my version) murdered Tamsen Donner and devoured her, was the last member of the party to be rescued. He and his hostile rescuers camp at night on their passage down the mountain at a site that earlier rescuers had used—including those who had rescued his wife and child. Propped by the campfire, exhausted, Keseberg notices a patch of calico sticking out of the snow and idly begins pulling on it: "It was larger than he had thought. He saw the pattern of the calico then and something broke loose in him and he stood and with both hands jerked on the calico and the frozen body of his daughter Ada sprang forth from the snow into his arms."

I intended that ending to invoke the ancient ending of tragic recognition, while at the same time suggesting that even such a monster as Lewis Keseberg deserves some measure of our pity. For the tragedy itself the ending seemed sufficient, but for the historical story there was the question of what happened to the survivors after their rescue. When I spoke to people about the story, they always asked me, and I wanted at least to hint that after great suffering human beings return to the quotidian, as we do. The omniscient voice telling the story—James Clyman peering down through the clouds—could certainly have simply gone on talking. But Keseberg's discovery of his daughter's body felt like a closure of that story; to go on talking about what happened afterward would turn tragedy into mere history.

I struggled with how to fit information about the aftermath into the structure I'd set up. First I tried writing a sort of "Where Are They Now" epilogue that would describe what happened to the Donner Party survivors. That felt slack compared to the tension of the central narrative. Worse, it turned black-humorous: Keseberg, for example, opened a restaurant, of which one rescuer told a friend, "I wouldn't want to eat there!" Nor did the Clymanesque narrative voice suit this merely reportorial assignment.

Then I saw that I could use some of the documentary material I'd collected to fill out the story. I added a new, very brief Part Five to the book after the Keseberg ending. It consisted of two statements, both contemporary and authentic, one by a journalist named Edwin Bryant, who had traveled with the Donners until they divided off from the main emigration beyond Fort Laramie (and who had successfully crossed the mountains into California himself), the other by Virginia Reed, a thirteen-year-old survivor. Bryant described the appalling scene at the mountain cabins the following June, 1847, when he accompanied a military party up from Sacramento, concluding, "The remains were ... collected and buried.... These melancholy duties to the dead being performed, the cabins, by order of Major

Swords, were fired, and with every thing surrounding them connected with this horrid and melancholy tragedy, were consumed."

Bryant's statement gave historical closure to the story, in a pedestrian voice something like the voice of the chorus in Greek tragedy. I still needed to indicate that the survivors recovered and got on with their lives. For that, Virginia Reed's droll description of her new life spoke volumes:

> *From a ranch in the Napa Valley Virginia Reed wrote* We are all very well pleased with California particulary with the climate let it be ever so hot a day thare is allwais cool nights it is a beautiful Country It is mostley in vallies it aut to be a beautiful Country to pay us for our trubel geting there

"Our trubel geting there," the last words in the book, encapsulate the whole story.

Similarly, with *The Making of the Atomic Bomb,* the logical place to end the story of the development of the first nuclear weapons was at Hiroshima in August 1945. Yet I had emphasized throughout my narrative the universal dilemma that the discovery of how to release nuclear energy posed humankind. Luckily, I found a document that managed to encompass both local and universal, a dream reported in the diary of a Japanese physician, Michihiko Hachiya, who had treated survivors at Hiroshima.

One of Hachiya's patients had reported seeing a man in the chaos after the atomic bombing holding his eyeball in his hand. The image had disturbed Hachiya's sleep and he had dreamed of that eye "sitting on the palm of a girl's hand. Suddenly it turned and leaped into the sky and then came flying back towards me, so that, looking up, I could see a great bare eyeball, bigger than life, hovering over my head, staring point blank at me. I was powerless to move." The great bare eyeball evoked the nuclear fireball. It evoked what Northrop Frye calls "the humiliation of being constantly watched by a hostile or derisive eye" that enraged Prometheus and that is characteristic of demonic tragedy, the kind of tragedy, Frye explains, "where we see or glimpse the undisplaced demonic vision, the vision of the *Inferno*."[18] The eyeball of Hachiya's dream evoked Emerson's "transparent eyeball" in his essay "Nature": "Standing on the bare ground . . . all mean egotism vanishes. I become a transparent eyeball; I am nothing; I see all; the currents of the Universal Being circulate through me; I am part or particle of God." After I quoted Hachiya's description of his iconic dream, then, I had only to add a few more words to end my book with an implied question:

> "I awakened short of breath and with my heart pounding," Michihiko Hachiya remembers.
>
> So do we all.

The implied question, of course, was *What are we going to do about it?*

Italo Calvino, the novelist, eulogizing the philosopher Roland Barthes, noted that Barthes sought to understand uniqueness through generalization. A critic comments of Calvino that he sought the opposite: to understand generalization through uniqueness.[19] Endings are a time for projecting generalization through uniqueness, through the local and the specific. Beginnings open out and start things going. Endings bring those things to closure. But at another, more symbolic level, endings also open out, into chambers connected to farther chambers, where the reverberations of your story activate universals. They're often what readers remember most vividly. They're your last chance to influence your reader before she goes away, back into her life.

However you end your story, congratulations on getting there. Every story you and I and the rest of our audacious company write is

a further initiation into an ancient and honorable craft, a craft that cuts windows through the terrifying opacity of the world.

Endings can also be beginnings. If you want to write, you can.

Glade
Summer 1994

NOTES

One: 'Words Like a Life Rope'

1. Cf. Elaine Scarry, *The Body in Pain* (Oxford University Press, 1985), pp. 305 ff.
2. Jonathan Shay, *Achilles in Vietnam* (Atheneum, 1994), p. 188.
3. Spinoza, *Ethics*, quoted in Viktor E. Frankl, *Man's Search for Meaning*, 4th ed. (Beacon Press, 1992), p. 82.
4. Ibid., p. 84.
5. Ibid., p. 85.
6. Roger Rosenblatt, "Rwanda Therapy," *New Republic*, 6 June 1994, pp. 14–16.
7. Shay, *Achilles*, p. 187.
8. "Death All Day in Kansas" appears in Richard Rhodes, *The Inland Ground* (Atheneum, 1970; rev. ed., University Press of Kansas, 1991).
9. Gertrude Stein, *The Making of Americans* (Harcourt Brace, 1934), p. 128.
10. Walt Whitman, "There Was a Child Went Forth," in Walt Whitman, *Complete Poetry and Collected Prose* (Library of America, 1982), p. 491 ff.

Two: Tools

1. Robert Pollack, *Signs of Life* (Houghton Mifflin, 1994), p. 2.
2. David Hubel, "Roger W. Sperry (1913–1994)," *Nature* 369 (19 May 1994): 186.

Three: Voices

1. Gabriel García Márquez, *Strange Pilgrims* (Knopf, 1993). Quoted in John Bayley, "Singing in the Rain," *New York Review of Books,* 17 February 1994, p. 21.
2. William Strunk, Jr., and E. B. White, *The Elements of Style,* 3rd ed. (Macmillan, 1979), p. 84.
3. Ibid., p. 70.
4. Ibid., p. 84.
5. Charles L. Camp, ed., *James Clyman, Frontiersman* (Champoeg Press, 1960), p. 228.
6. Richard Rhodes, *The Ungodly* (Charterhouse Books, 1973), pp. 196–97.
7. Mary Catherine Bateson, *Composing a Life* (Atlantic Monthly Press, 1989), p. 34.
8. Herman Melville, *Moby-Dick* (University of California Press, 1979), p. 2.
9. Ibid., p. 248.
10. Richard Rhodes, *Holy Secrets* (Doubleday, 1978), p. 1.
11. Richard Rhodes, *The Making of the Atomic Bomb* (Simon & Schuster, 1986), p. 14.
12. Ibid., p. 13.
13. Quoted in Suzannah Lessard, "The Present Moment," *The New Yorker,* 13 April 1987, p. 57.

Four: Research

1. Lionel Trilling, *The Liberal Imagination* (Harcourt Brace Jovanovich, 1978), p. 194.
2. Barbara Small Hamilton, *The Hidden Legacy* (Fort Bragg CA: Cypress House, 1992).
3. Bateson, *Composing a Life,* pp. 36–7.
4. Rhodes, *Atomic Bomb,* p. 275.
5. E. Annie Proulx, quoted in Sara Rimer, "At Midlife, a Novelist Is Born," *New York Times,* 23 June 1994, p. C10.
6. Richard Rhodes, *A Hole in the World* (Simon & Schuster, 1990), p. 52.

Five: The Shape of Things to Come: I

1. Northrop Frye, *Anatomy of Criticism* (Princeton University Press, 1957), p. 310.
2. Richard Rhodes, *The Last Safari* (Doubleday, 1980), pp. 3–7.

Six: The Shape of Things to Come: II

1. Ingmar Bergman, *Images: My Life in Film* (Arcade, 1994), quoted in Michael Meyer, "The Magician," *New York Review of Books* 41 (11): 18.
2. Richard Rhodes, "Atomic Logic," *Rolling Stone*, 24 February 1994, p. 30.
3. Richard Rhodes, "How I Rode with Harold Lewis on a Diesel Freight Train Down to Gridley, Kansas, and Back," *Audience*, March/April 1971. Reprint, Rhodes, *Looking for America* (Doubleday, 1979).
4. Richard Rhodes, "The Last Kennedy," *Audience*, November/December 1971. Reprint, *Looking for America.*

Seven: Editing

1. Leopold Infeld, quoted in Rhodes, *Atomic Bomb*, p. 196.
2. Sallie Tisdale, *Talk Dirty To Me* (Doubleday, 1994), pp. 37–38.

Eight: Business

1. Gertrude Stein, *Everybody's Autobiography*, quoted in Paul William Kingston and Jonathan R. Cole, *The Wages of Writing* (Columbia University Press, 1986), p. xiii.
2. Kingston and Cole, *Wages of Writing*, p. 57.
3. Ibid.
4. Ibid., pp. 163 ff.
5. Frye, *Anatomy*, p. 104.
6. Jon Katz, "The Tales They Tell in Cyber-Space Are a Whole Other Story," *New York Times*, 23 January 1994, Arts and Leisure, p. 1.
7. Ibid.
8. Larry Brown, *On Fire* (Algonquin Books of Chapel Hill, 1994), p. viii.
9. Sarah Lyall, "Book Notes," *New York Times*, 29 June 1994, p. C21.

Nine: Other Voices

1. Anthony Trollope, *An Autobiography* (Dodd, Mead, 1927), p. 21.
2. Quoted in Readings, *Harper's,* November 1993, p. 34.
3. Andrew Delbanco, "Necropolis News," *New Republic,* 18 and 25 July 1994, p. 47.
4. Iris Murdoch, *Metaphysics as a Guide to Morals* (Chatto & Windus, 1992), p. 169.
5. Norman Sims, *The Literary Journalists* (Ballantine, 1984), p. 24.
6. Sharon O'Brien, "My Willa Cather: How Writing Her Story Shaped My Own," *The New York Times Book Review,* 20 February 1994, pp. 3 ff.
7. Trollope, *Autobiography,* p. 1.
8. Ibid., pp. 24–25.
9. Ibid., pp. 59–60.
10. Ibid., p. 63.
11. Ibid., p. 61.
12. Ibid., p. 85.
13. Ibid., pp. 88–89.
14. Ibid., pp. 91–92.
15. Ibid., pp. 202–3.
16. Ibid., pp. 103–6.
17. Quoted in Jonathan Keates, "Anthony Trollope," in Justin Wintle, ed., *Makers of Nineteenth Century Culture* (Routledge & Kegan Paul, 1982), p. 634.
18. Charles E. Modlin, ed., *Certain Things Last: The Selected Short Stories of Sherwood Anderson* (Four Walls Eight Windows, 1992).
19. Richard Rhodes, "The Death of the Everglades," in *Looking for America,* p. 59.

Ten: Bottom

1. Quoted in Rhodes, *Atomic Bomb,* p. 16.
2. Brown, *On Fire,* p. vii.
3. Pollack, *Signs of Life,* pp. 11–12.
4. Ibid., pp. 176 ff.
5. Edward O. Wilson, *Naturalist* (Island Press, 1994), pp. 212–13.
6. Ibid., p. 213.
7. Robert Sternberg, quoted in Bruce Fellman, "This Thing Called Love," *Yale Alumni Magazine,* February 1994, p. 26.

8. Ibid., pp. 28–29.
9. Reproduced from Theodore Modis, *Predictions* (Simon & Schuster, 1992), p. 240.
10. Ibid., p. 35.
11. Ibid., pp. 73–74.
12. Ibid., p. 76.
13. Ibid., p. 77.
14. Ibid., p. 82.
15. Ibid., p. 246.
16. Ibid., p. 247.
17. Robert Frost, "Ten Mills II. The Span of Life," in *The Poetry of Robert Frost* (Henry Holt, 1979), p. 308.
18. Frye, *Anatomy*, pp. 222–23.
19. Michael Wood, "Agile Among the Tombs," *New York Review of Books*, 14 July 1994, p. 15.

INDEX

INDEX

INDEX

INDEX

INDEX

INDEX

INDEX